RECIPES FOR THE HEART
MORSELS FOR THE SOUL

An Invitation to Life, Love, and Wellness
With a Cookbook for
Delicious Healthy Eating

By Carol Anne Pock, B.A., Ed.

Heartbeat Publishing
Arlington, TX

Published by Heartbeat Publishing

P.O. Box 171813, Arlington, TX 76003-1813

Printed in the United States of America

Pock, Carol Anne, BA, Ed.

co-author: Pock, Les

Recipes For The Heart, Morsels For The Soul

ISBN 0-9671975-0-3

Editing & graphic design
by

Schmidt, Kaye & Co.

Cover design by Ron Kaye

DEDICATION

I dedicate this book to Les, the man in my life who allowed me to grow in ways that enriched my life, and whose influence and unending love allowed me to understand "real living". Because he chose life, the love for healthy living became my life. Les' love and support has sustained me through the completion of this project. Thank you for having the most "finicky" taste buds…which challenged me to discover and experience the real joy that comes from eating "heart-healthy".

Your love for Family is my constant motivation for healthy living. Thank you for that gift.

I Love You!

ACKNOWLEDGMENTS

Without the support of many, I would not have had the vision to inspire others to follow a path toward better health. I would like to thank the following people for being an influential part of my life:

Les Pock — whose presence in my life is a gift that I cherish every day, and who assisted me through every facet of developing this book with his relentless guidance, his clear vision of success, an obsession for excellence, discriminating taste buds, and his need for an abundance of moist, dense foods. Most importantly, I am grateful for his ongoing love and support for me, and a crystal clear vision of maintaining health and happiness throughout his lifetime.

Howie and Jackie Pock — for being the two most wonderful and supportive children a low-fat chef could ever ask for, and for their patience and understanding of the many hours spent producing this book. Your love reminds me every day of the precious gift that is our life.

Larry and Gayle Weinstein — for the encouragement and devotion you gave me every step of the way, making this dream a reality.

Jennifer Weinstein — whose refreshing young love and energy inspire me to recognize all the great benefits of healthy living.

Marilyn Boskind — for typing, tasting, and keeping me on track whenever necessary.

Dr. Arnold Pock — for acting as technical editor, medical consultant, and a strong proponent of healthy, happy "family" living.

Dr. Arnyce Pock — for her personal ongoing medical advice and moral support.

Wayne Whitcomb, Rabbi Keith Stern and Dr. Neil Rosen for always being there.

THANK YOU TO THE FOLLOWING CONTRIBUTORS:

- ♥ Sabina Kamen-Handel
- ♥ Phil Handel
- ♥ Vivian Pock
- ♥ Rose Schwartz
- ♥ Karen Danielson
- ♥ Pam Margules Mark
- ♥ Rabbi Keith Stern
- ♥ Lynda & Jeff Friedensohn
- ♥ Drs. Arlene and Mark Schwartz
- ♥ Kristel Carter
- ♥ Phil & Wendy Geisler
- ♥ Cookie Kabakoff
- ♥ The "Cooking With Care" Weight Management Group Participants
- ♥ Rochelle Wolfe
- ♥ Julie Berman
- ♥ Elsa Leveton
- ♥ Dawn Freeman
- ♥ Megan Kuehl
- ♥ Dr. Kathy Bailey
- ♥ Rabbi Jeffrey Kaye
- ♥ Dr. Patrick Kobett, our family physician, whose genuine personal care could never be paralleled
- ♥ Dr. Gary Donovitz, a great physician and a true friend
- ♥ Ron Kaye and Connie Schmidt, who were so much more than just editors.

My thanks to all of you for sharing the attitude and for your enthusiasm toward living longer and better.

FOREWORD

There is an old Jewish story:

On the way back to his palace, a king encountered carriage troubles. He had to alight from his beautiful coach while repairs were made. Looking around the remote area where he was temporarily stranded, the king spotted a rundown home. There was smoke coming out of the chimney, and the unmistakably delicious aroma of fresh baking wafted through the air. The king was cold and hungry – and he *was* the king – so he and his bodyguards approached the little house and knocked. The door opened and there before them stood a woman in an apron stained by years of cooking and cleaning.

"Oh, my! Oh, your majesty! I am humbled to stand before you. Oh, and look at me! I beg your pardon, dear king…"

"Oh please, Madam, don't apologize to me. My carriage has broken and while it's being fixed, I prefer to wait someplace warm. Please forgive the imposition." The king dismissed his guards as the woman, whose name was Hiya, hastily shooed the cats off the old chair in the main room. When he was seated in the old chair, the woman brought the king a steaming plate. "Please, your Majesty, try my noodle

…To every thing I cook, I add love.

kugel. It's a sweet noodle pudding. It's my own recipe."

To make a long story short, the king loved it. He had never tasted anything like it — so delicate, so sweet, so satisfying. After eating three helpings, he got up and called his scribe to write down the recipe so that the royal chef could duplicate the amazing dish. With the recipe recorded, the king took another piece of the kugel and walked back to the carriage, now ready to roll.

The royal chef dutifully took the recipe the king delivered to him, and the next day he prepared the kugel. The king took a bite. "It's good," he said. "But it's not as good as the old woman's kugel. Try it again!" Well, after three attempts to replicate the recipe, the royal chef still couldn't please the king. Perhaps, the chef mused, this woman purposely left out an ingredient to shame him or to keep her dish a secret. So he went to the king's guards and asked where the old woman lived. With map in hand, the chef searched out the woman named Hiya, whose cooking was causing him concern about the future of his job.

When the chef tracked her down, he demanded that Hiya share her true recipe. She smiled sweetly while shrugging her shoulders. "But, I told the man every ingredient I use and the amounts. Come, I'll show you what I do. I'll make a kugel right in front of you." And as Hiya mixed the eggs with the cream and the sugar and the cheese and the cinnamon, and as she boiled the egg noodles, then drained them and mixed all the ingredients together, throwing it all into the oven, the chef was dumbfounded. For everything that Hiya did was exactly the same thing the chef did: same measurements, same ingredients, same everything. Well, maybe off a teaspoon here or there, but really very insignificant differences. If this was the case, then what was so different about hers? When it came out of the oven and the chef tasted it, he found that, indeed, hers was superior.

Recipes For The Heart, Morsels For The Soul

Dejectedly he said to Hiya, "I just don't understand. Why is yours better? Is it the eggs? The noodles? The age of the oven or the pan? What makes yours so much better?"

The old woman placed her hand on the chef's shoulder. "There is one ingredient in my kugel that is not in yours."

"Tell me, please, Hiya! I watched you the whole time! What is in your kugel that's not in mine?"

"To everything I cook, I add love."

Carol Pock adds love to everything she cooks. Her recipes are created from a place of care and concern for the well-being and happiness of all people. She knows how food satisfies. And Carol knows how healthy food nurtures the soul. Carol has learned about nurturing the body and the soul in the trenches of illness and anxiety. She's no naïve diet book writer or fad follower. She knows, up close and personally, about healing and prayer – and action.

This book isn't about sitting back passively and waiting for someone to come to the rescue. It's all about taking action and taking responsibility. Just ask Carol, and she'll tell you. You want a healthier life, a life of quality and no self-deception? Carol can help show you the way, but ultimately, it is up to you.

I was honored to be Carol Pock's rabbi for eleven years. She taught me things about health and eating and self-esteem and mind games that stay locked in my head. I hope you'll let her into your life as well. You won't be disappointed with this book. If you read it and absorb it, Carol might just help you change your life for the better. Hiya's — I mean, Carol's — book may just be what you need. Let her add some love to your life.

Rabbi Keith Stern

PREFACE:
A CHANGE OF HEART

We are ordinary people, probably a lot like you. We didn't start out intending to be crusaders for any significant cause. We were busy living and enjoying our lives while building our dreams. We always enjoyed tasty foods, and never gave a second thought to what we put into our bodies. After all, we thought that there was nothing wrong with the things we enjoyed, and if they were fattening, it didn't show on us. We ate many of the same things that our parents had eaten, never considering the long-term effects.

...eating and living healthy can be as delicious and joyous as you want it to be.

It was only when my husband Les was faced with a life-threatening condition, brought about in great part by the types of foods he ate, that we began giving serious thought to our daily eating habits. We never considered giving up the foods that brought us great pleasure and satisfaction. Furthermore, we had little desire to replace our tasty, high-fat foods with a flavorless regimen. But when CRISIS became our household word, we committed ourselves to the changes necessary to survive, while holding fast to our desire for living freely. What we ultimately found was a life filled with great satisfaction, pleasure and *foods with fabulous flavor!*

Following our mind-awakening encounter, we grew excited about sharing what we experienced. But for you, my readers... all of you... read on now, before you have to become a student in the accelerated class for healthy living, the class that people are *dying* to get into! Most of all, I want to reassure you that *eating and living healthy can be as delicious and joyous as you want it to be.* It simply takes a refreshed understanding of your priorities, combined with a renewed awareness of how your body functions.

It is important to realize that everyone can create a lifestyle that is fulfilling as well as healthy. So do read on, for health and joy are what this book has to offer!

As with any significant lifestyle change, this one will take time, dedication, information, and a positive vision of success. And keep in mind that the recipes in this book were developed by a woman who had the desire — the "why" — but lacked the technique — the "how". I discovered that it takes a firm commitment to learn, understand, and practice both. The contents of this book were developed to make it easier for you to accomplish both the *understanding of the why,* and the *actual practice of the how.*

You can use these recipes as they are presented, or incorporate them into your menus as meal-makeovers. Whether you are an experienced soüs chef or a novice cook, I am sure you will find the recipes easy to follow. Let these recipes, along with the additional "morsels" of knowledge and techniques, help lead you into a new lifestyle of eating primarily for the health of it. It just may grant you a *longer lifetime!*

Throughout the text, I have included references to the recipes, which are located in a separate section toward the back of the book. You will also find, at the very end of the book, a comprehensive index of all the recipes to assist you in finding a specific dish that tantalizes your imagination.

May you eat well and live long!

Carol

CONTENTS

CHAPTER ONE:
GOOD TIMES... COME ON, LET'S CELEBRATE

During his high school and college days, my husband Les was into body-building. He felt great and looked good, and was always proud of his strength and physique. As with many of us, however, the years passed and Les found himself focusing upon other priorities.

Les was going to turn 40 in September of 1991, and I was planning a surprise birthday party. Close relatives, some from great distances, flew in to attend. The formula for this successful celebration was what I called The "Four F's": *Food, Family, Friends, and Fun!* Notice the order in which I *assumed* these were valued.

I arranged for a casual party at a local bowling alley, as Les is always happiest when he is physically active. I knew that having everyone share this event, while participating in a sport, would surely put the "happy" into his birthday. Moreover, Les always loved to eat, so choosing food for the party was the easy part. I ordered one of his many favorites: barbecue. The restaurant I hired to cater the party specialized in tender smoked brisket, creamy coleslaw, beans, French-fries, onion rings, and all the Texas fixin's — things that were certain to bring a smile to Les' face.

The party was a smashing success, and Les turned 40, filled with confidence and zeal about the next phase of his life.

...It was only yesterday that Les seemed totally healthy! Fear and uncertainty had now invaded our once-calm and happy lifestyle.

Clouds On The Horizon

September through February passed normally and quietly... or at least as quietly as can be expected for a couple with two young children. As with most of our fellow baby boomers, we thought we were traveling down the path of health, happiness, and prosperity. We were happy with our lives, and confident about our visions of the future.

Les had not done a great deal of structured exercising since college age. As a matter of fact, except for playing baseball in an adult league and a few other occasional minor activities, he had not engaged in significant physical activity on a routine basis. He was, however, beginning to have a yearning to get back into better physical condition.

We had just built a new home, our "dream house". Les planned to put exercise equipment in our upstairs recreation room. The builder had constructed the house according to Les' specifications, including additional floor support for his workout area. Les purchased a treadmill and a universal weight machine to complement his free weights that had been left sitting dormant.

Before beginning his new exercise program, Les thought it might be wise to have a complete physical examination, especially since he had just passed the big four-oh. Now, don't get me wrong; Les is certainly no more responsible about his health than the average American male, but he couldn't avoid considering all the new information about heart disease that was appearing in the media on a near-daily basis. A physician's approval before undertaking any new fitness program was repeatedly recommended. Les decided it would be a good idea to heed the recommendation, even though he was certain, of course, that there was nothing wrong with him.

Quite often, people tend to avoid various medical exams or tests if they are in fear of learning that they have a health problem. It is often said that most men take better care of their cars than they do their own bodies, and Les could have qualified as a member of that club. In fact, aside from his renewed desire to recover his old "Mr. Muscle" physique, putting his health on the front burner was not always his first interest.

After his check-up in October of 1991, Les planned to make an appointment for a stress test. Like many people, he kept postponing his appointment for the treadmill test, due to other priorities. But was it only because of his "other priorities", or was Les just sure that he was fine? He had already started lifting weights and running, and it wasn't until early February of 1992, after about four months of procrastination, that Les finally had his stress test.

The Storm Breaks

I had been a special education teacher for our local Arlington, Texas school district for many years. On the day of Les' stress test, he called me at school, asking me to meet him at home. There was an uncomfortable edge to his voice. When I arrived home, Les told me to sit down. He related that during his stress test, he had only walked on the treadmill for a short time when he lightheartedly asked the doctor, "So how does it look? Pretty good, huh?"

The doctor shook his head and, in his professional but calm tone, quickly answered, "No." He then abruptly ordered the nurse to "stop the machine... immediately."

The doctor informed Les that he had seen abnormalities indicating there were major coronary arterial blockages. An immediate angiogram would be necessary to locate the exact points of obstruction. To say the least, Les was in shock.

As he told me the news, his words seemed like a big blur. I too was shocked and stunned. My proud warrior, in the absolute prime of his life, was in real danger. *He had never experienced any symptoms whatsoever,* and neither of us had any clue that a problem could have existed.

Les detailed the doctor's explanation about the medical procedure that would have to be done immediately. Knowing little about heart disease, I found my mind swimming with visions of a heart attack or bypass surgery. I grew very quiet and fearful, and, with teary eyes, asked what the next step would be. Les told me that he had another appointment with the doctor the following day and was instructed to take things very slow and easy until then. Apparently the doctor felt that Les' condition might be severe enough that even mild exertion, such as climbing stairs, could be dangerous.

I called the principal at the school where I was teaching to let him know what had occurred. He shared with me that he knew a number of people, including his own father, who had undergone major heart procedures and had done very well. Even though I knew he was only trying to calm me, the conversation had in fact left me upset. I realized that all the people he was describing were older, and Les was far too young to be compared to seniors. To think of Les as compared to a group of elderly people only exaggerated my newfound fears that he might, indeed, be mortal.

Shadows From The Past

In the midst of our anxiety and confusion it occurred to me that there were certain similarities to the loss I suffered in my own childhood. When I was 12 years old, I lost my father, Jack Kamen, to heart disease. During the prior year, my family decided to take a driving trip out west, heading to the Grand Canyon from Chicago. As we approached Wyoming, my father started to feel dizzy, and experienced some breathing difficulties at the higher altitude.

Now, remember that in 1967, much less was known about heart disease or the symptoms indicating a blocked vessel. My father tried to continue driving in spite of his discomfort, but as we neared Newcastle, he had to be hospitalized. Once there, it was discovered that my father had suffered a stroke. My mother hired a gentleman to drive our car back to

Chicago, and our family flew home. Little did we know that this experience was really the beginning of the end for a man who we naturally thought would live forever.

The next few months were very difficult for my father, and, at age 50, he ultimately lost his life to heart disease. I went to school on a Friday morning, only to return that afternoon to learn that he had become seriously ill. On Saturday, the very next day, he passed away. Because there was little known about heart disease or its prevention, at the age of twelve, I was left with only one parent.

These painful memories from my past began to flood back into my present, and I imagined the only future I could... the only outcome I was familiar with. It's remarkable how a frightening situation faced in adult life can so frequently rekindle the fears and doubts left over from childhood.

So many agonizing questions were swirling through our minds as Les and I faced this frightening new page in our lives. I had to focus upon Les' well being, for now he needed my strength, not my doubts. How did this young healthy couple suddenly find themselves in such a serious situation?

Still in shock over the whole matter, Les and I spoke about the possible outcome. We also discussed financial and household issues, and took care of important business and family details. We were both trying, without actually coming out and saying the words, to come to grips with the fact that he could die, if not now, in the near future. Our fears, even the unspoken ones, hung over all of us like a dark and foreboding cloud. After all, it was only yesterday that Les seemed totally healthy! Fear and uncertainty had now invaded our once-calm and happy lifestyle.

CHAPTER TWO:
DISCOVERY

The doctor scheduled Les for an immediate heart catheterization (angiogram). One thing became certain: health had to become our priority. More realistically, everything now would depend on it... thinking of our two young children reminded us of that.

The angiogram showed two blockages. Les had one artery that was almost completely closed off and one that was approximately 45 percent obstructed. Diagnosis: arteriosclerosis — a major build-up of fatty plaque creating a narrowing — or in this case, practically a complete closure — of the right coronary artery.

Les was a candidate for "PTCA" (Percutaneous Transluminal Coronary Angioplasty). When successfully completed, this procedure enables the blood to flow freely once again, thus providing the vital oxygen and nutrients to the heart. Generally, if the vessel then remains open for at least six months, a routine of proper diet and exercise would likely prevent reoccurrence of the blockage for a long time. As follow-up, regular treadmill (stress) EKG tests would be necessary to monitor the integrity of the repair and the condition of the other arteries over the life-long term.

We traveled to Houston to have Doctor Milton Klein perform the balloon angioplasty at The Methodist Hospital. We were fortunate to have this luxury, as managed care had not yet taken over. In addition to the medical

I could not help thinking about the possibility that Les may not live long enough to help his four-year-old daughter and seven-year-old son grow up.

history that Les had furnished, Dr. Klein asked many questions about his past eating habits, food selections, and exercise and work patterns. After integrating the assessment of Les' history and past lifestyle with his evaluation of the catheterization film, the doctor drew two conclusions. One was that with the early onset of cardiovascular disease, the condition was worsened, if not principally caused, *by many years of a high-fat diet*. Second, the level of the blockage indicated that Les was likely only two to four weeks away from a major heart attack! With nothing whatsoever to suggest a potential problem, it was like a miraculous stroke of luck to have caught this so close to the inevitable disastrous outcome.

Just before Les went into surgery for the angioplasty, he handed the doctor a short note our young son Howie had written, saying that he hoped his dad wouldn't die, and that he would come home soon. Les wanted the doctor to know that he had two young children waiting for his return.

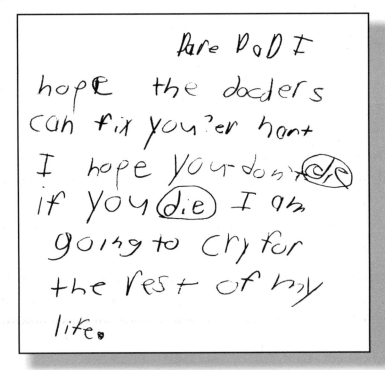

Recipes For The Heart, Morsels For The Soul

During the angioplasty, my sister and I stayed in the waiting room. It was apparent that I was easily the youngest person there. Most of the others waiting for a report on their spouses were considerably older. It felt as if we were struck by a disease more common among the elderly.

I could not help thinking about the possibility that Les may not live long enough to help his four-year-old daughter and seven-year-old son grow up. This terrifying image was hard to shake. We all were beginning to realize how we had taken good health for granted.

The Procedure

The PTCA begins with a small incision made in the vicinity of the femoral artery on one side of the groin. A sheath is then inserted as a guide through the incision site to create an opening path. A long wire is fed through the sheath into the artery, and is threaded all the way up to the heart. By watching video monitors, it is carefully steered through the winding turns and curves into the blood vessels supplying the heart. On the lead end of the wire is a narrow, deflated balloon-like device. When the area of the blockage is approached, the balloon is carefully moved forward into the portion obstructed by the plaque. Using a type of externally controlled pump, the balloon is then inflated (usually more than once), compressing the plaque outward against the walls of the vessel, thus re-opening the area to allow blood to flow once again. During the inflation, there is a complete cut-off of the blood supply to the heart from that particular vessel. As a result, it is not unusual to experience the actual symptoms of a real heart attack, such as chest pain, pressure, shortness of breath, or even the feeling that an elephant has suddenly chosen to use your chest as his easy chair.

The procedure took about fifty minutes, but the recovery would last several hours. This period was critical, because Les would have to lie flat on his back, while medical personnel applied constant heavy pressure to the entry site until the bleeding stopped. Careful monitoring of heart activity would be ongoing for the duration of recovery.

Once again, we were lucky. The procedure was successful the first time. The hours to follow were filled with some relief, and yet some worry about the road ahead. After my sister Gayle and I had lunch at the Medical Center, I spent the rest of the day in the hospital reading books about heart disease. I wanted to begin to acquire a better understanding of where we were to go from here.

Our doctor was also a teacher of sorts, prescribing the best medicine for wellness and prevention. He explained that the maintenance of health in the face of CVD (cardiovascular disease) was very much left up to us. Knowing the "how" and "why" was the key to unlocking our door to a healthy future. He warned us of the dangers of denial, and explained the importance of self-monitoring. Early detection is very often the key to saving one's life, whether afflicted with heart disease, many forms of cancer, or various other illnesses.

Les' recovery from the procedure went smoothly. On the second and final day in the hospital, he was visited by the dietitian for a short consultation. I was there at the time, and remember that she gave us two basic important points:

(1)   Eat only a maximum of 30 grams of fat per day, and

(2)   Never consume anything with noticeable saturated fat, or foods that include the word "hydrogenized" or "hydrogenated" in the list of ingredients. (See Chapter 11 for more information on hydrogenated fats.)

As to what it all meant and how to practically apply this information on a day to day level… we did not have a clue. Les was discharged from the hospital into the beginning of a lifestyle change that was to be forever — one way or another.

Les and I were not used to having such little control over events in our lives. Being unaccustomed to waiting for life to happen, I began actively participating in "the business of regaining health". I hadn't yet realized how successful we could be. But the road toward improved health appeared, at first, as a maze. Later, it turned out to be amazing!

CHAPTER THREE:
NEW BEGINNINGS

At first, Les and I found ourselves sitting in our kitchen wondering, "What will we eat tonight?" That was only the beginning. What about all the rest of the meals that lay ahead…tomorrow and beyond? From that point forward, we became self-taught self-starters in healthful fat-free living. To ensure the best odds of keeping Les' vessels open, we were determined to learn all about the fat in food. Les would need to base his eating habits upon that newfound knowledge, and maintain them permanently. We understood that he would have to change his lifestyle and his diet forever.

...we set out to learn everything that we could about the human heart: what makes it tick, what keeps it healthy, and what is responsible for harming it. I knew that knowledge is power...

Embarking upon our own personal quest, we set out to learn everything that we could about the human heart: what makes it tick, what keeps it healthy, and what is responsible for harming it. I knew that knowledge is power, and that a clear understanding of how Les ended up in this over-crowded boat would be one of the tools needed to stay afloat.

Even though there had been many advances in the diagnosis, treatment, and prevention of heart disease since my father had died, I realize now that neither of us knew much more about healthy eating than my own parents had. I recalled that at one time earlier that year while driving into Dallas, I passed a sign advertising a well-known purveyor of prime Midwestern steaks. I remembered that seven years earlier, my sister had found an outlet in Houston and, as a gift, sent Les a package of prime-cut steaks, much to his delight. Years later, I was to discover that this most sumptuous cut of meat was also one of the most unhealthy. Even the slightest marbling of fat that added flavor turned out to be a "prime" culprit in causing the problem Les was having. A history of poor choices had caught up with us, and much earlier than we would have ever imagined.

Our local cardiologist made the suggestion that we consider becoming vegetarians, or at least avoid red meat at all cost. At that time, such advice seemed to be quite extreme, and considering Les' food obsession, it was virtually shocking! Later, we came to understand the intention: to move positively toward a lifestyle change that might improve his chance for a longer life span. While we never quite planned to be strict vegetarians, we at least had a ball to run with.

Our search for information led us to confirm the only likely cause of Les' problem. Since he had no immediate family history predisposing him to heart disease through genetics, it almost certainly was related to his diet. For some time now, we have all been hearing about the cardiovascular dangers of red meat and fried foods, but Les and I, at least, had never really understood the physiological relationship between heart disease and foods with saturated fats. Now we were starting to realize the extent of the damage that dietary fat could cause.

All tissues in the body need oxygen and other nutrients in the blood to thrive and survive. The blood is circulated by the heart, which pumps approximately 100,000 times daily to deliver and recycle this nourishment throughout the body. The adult heart (which is shaped like an egg and is about the size of a clenched fist) does its job by circulating roughly five liters of blood through approximately 60,000 miles of vessels. But what about the needs of the heart itself? After all, it requires the same oxygen and nutrients as any other muscle or vital organ, or it will quickly begin to deteriorate and die.

The coronary arteries are responsible for feeding the heart muscle. Any interruption in the flow of oxygen-rich blood results in the heart being severely compromised, and subsequently damaged or even destroyed. Most fatal heart attacks are the result of a sudden, extreme deprivation of these elements, particularly oxygen. What gives heart disease the name "Silent Killer" is the unfortunate fact that in an alarming number of cases, there are no symptoms or indications of any potential problems, prior to death. Your first and only symptom could be a fatal one.

Our highest goal in offering this book is the attempt to save lives. As of this writing, the statistics from the World Health Organization tell us that more than *12 million* people die *each year* from cardiovascular disease. In the United States alone, according to the American Heart Association, almost *half of all deaths* are caused by this silent killer. This translates to almost *as many* deaths as from *all other causes combined*, including cancer and all other illnesses and accidents. The staggering number of over 250,000 cardiac-related deaths occur every year before the victim has a chance to reach the hospital. It is our sincere hope that we will soon realize a reduction in these numbers.

There are, of course, other risk factors beside fats in the blood. Cigarette smoke, lack of physical activity, and high blood pressure can also be significant contributors. Usually, men are slightly more prone to early onset than women, due to hormonal differences. Heredity and advancing age can also play a part, as can obesity. Many of these red flags can be detected. Medicine, however, is more of an art than an exact science. Even with extensive medical diagnostic testing, there is no absolute crystal ball. We must commit ourselves to the effort of reducing the risks that are within our control.

Remember that Les never experienced any symptoms, and had no history that would indicate a potential for the early onset of heart disease. He had no major risk factors. He was never a smoker or a drinker, and was not overweight. The harsh reality he would have to accept is that diet can and does play a major role in one's health, even in the absence of other risk factors.

Les was determined to follow the new rules, and he decided never to take his health for granted again. After the angioplasty, he was to be stress-tested in two weeks, and again in six weeks. Another check-up would follow again in six months, including a repeat cardiac catheterization. Examinations by a cardiologist would be necessary annually for the rest of his life. If the vessels stayed open over a long term, the combination of exercise and his significantly improved diet would offer a good chance that the repaired vessel could be successfully maintained. Hopefully, then, Les could look forward to many more years.

CHAPTER FOUR:
BABY STEPS

By now you know that when people speak about fat and the ill effects it has on the heart, they are referring to "dietary fat" — fat consumed in the foods we eat. Our journey to healthier eating began with a three-hour grocery shopping trip. We started reading everything we could get our hands on, every label on every product that captured our interest. We stocked up on all the available fat-free products. Bear in mind, however, that this was in 1992. The fat-free market was just beginning to break open, so the pickings were pretty slim. At that time, there was also a bit of confusion about the various types of fats, and how one could interpret the true low-down based solely upon the labeling of many products.

Even though Les knew that it was now necessary to adopt a strict new approach to eating, you can certainly understand the difficulty he had with this new discipline. After all, he had lived 40 years. For approximately the last 30, he had been accustomed to eating his fill of whatever foods turned him on. As thrilled as he was to be alive, he would occasionally feel frustrated or deprived, as he struggled to force his logic to prevail over temptation. At times, his struggle even became downright depressing.

I was most concerned about whether this man who, for all practical purposes, "lived to eat", would really be able

...A potential life-or-death situation does not ask if you can, but rather says, "You can."

to adjust to such a change in lifestyle in order to regain his health. In most areas, Les has always shown above-average common sense and deductive reasoning. What we were now dealing with, however, was the necessity to control a behavior that didn't *feel* dangerous, yet threatened his very life.

A potential life-or-death situation does not ask *if* you can, but rather says, "*You can.*" Still, I was skeptical about whether he would really ever be able to give up the high-fat foods he loved, even knowing that they were actually killing him. And would I be able to help motivate him to make these changes and stick with them? Would I have to cajole, even force him? Or would I have to always look over his shoulder, personally seeing to it that he adhered to what was (in his mind) a completely alien lifestyle? These were some of the impending concerns that filled me with doubts and more worries as we took our first baby steps towards a healthier lifestyle.

CHAPTER FIVE:
A DOUBLE TRIUMPH

Although Les was fully *obsessed with*, and had an insatiable appetite for, the taste of most high-fat foods, he surprised us all. In fact, knowing the true depth of his desires, it was almost a shock that he not only started eating healthier full-force, but kept it up unwaveringly! He took in almost no fat, and ran 30 to 60 minutes every other day. From these changes alone, he actually lost well over 20 pounds during the first two months. But how did he maintain such self-control? Addictions are typically difficult to beat, even with outside help. What was it, I wondered, that gave him this incredibly uncharacteristic ability?

Les and I learned that improving our health is truly an act of love, and that without good health, nothing else matters.

Truthfully, I had another personal reason for wanting to know the answer to that question. You see, like many people, I too had a vice: shopping. On many occasions, it had reached the point of creating many more problems than pleasures. Though shopping might seem to be merely an enjoyable activity, the urge to splurge was not something that I could simply turn off like a light switch. One night a few years after his diagnosis, I finally asked Les the question, not realizing his answer would be the simple secret that many people are searching for. I asked him, "How do you do it? How have you been able to maintain such perfect self-discipline after more than three years of this? I've seen so many other people in similar situations fall off track. How can you possibly have such control all the time, especially in the face of constant temptation?"

It was obvious by Les' response that he had started to dig deeply into his soul to understand the connection between life and death, between what was important and what was not.

"I guess I was just forced into looking more closely and honestly at my priorities," he replied. "You know how much I love to eat. On some level, I think that I had actually begun to define how happy I was by the things I ate. When I found out that I was in real trouble, I got hit in the face with the realization that the times I've shared with you and the kids meant more to me than any meal ever could, no matter how delicious.

"When I really thought about it, even the idea of never being able to eat the things I enjoyed most seemed secondary to the thought of being torn away from my family, which was far more devastating. No amount of instant gratification could relieve the fear of being taken away from you and the kids.

"Our children are magnificent, and I want to be here to watch them grow into even more accomplished adults, and to help guide them and share in their joy. I love you and the two of them so much that it isn't even a question of fighting temptation. Instead, it's the overwhelming desire to spend longer and healthier lives together that gives me the strength I need to maintain my new attitude."

He paused a moment and continued, "The funny thing is, when I finally realized my true priorities, I actually began to enjoy, and even prefer, the taste of healthier foods. Obviously, there are times when I'm with other people, and they're offering me things to eat that aren't consistent with my 'lifestyle', that I feel tempted — especially if I'm hungry. But whenever that happens, all I have to do is focus on the thought of the four of us staying together, and it works magic every time. *That* hunger (for family) is stronger than any temptation that can be put on a plate in front of me. And when I explain to people why I'm not 'chowing down' like I used to, it just serves to remind me, all over again, how much you all mean to me, and it makes my resolve even more firm. It also further supports my efforts to exercise, even though it sometimes gets grueling. I never really enjoyed running before, but now it feels like I'm doing something important, for the best reasons I can imagine. I'm taking control of my life, and I will not let a piece of fried chicken get in the way."

He then went on, "Remember the theme of the movie *Hook*? When Peter Pan recognized that his purpose in life — his happy thought — was his family, he suddenly found that he really could fly. I can now relate to the truth in that, and in my own way, I guess I've learned to fly, too."

Les' response that night actually helped me to find the self-control I needed to overcome my shopping fetish, and to exercise it ever since.

Heart And Soul

One day, as the children were eating pizza, I noticed that the usual covetous look in Les' eyes was missing. That look (or, rather, the absence of it) really hit home, and illustrated what he had shared about his strength of purpose. I realized from his expression that this could not just be about Les changing his diet. It was imperative that our entire family embrace health. Thus, it was Les who became my motivation to learn and teach others, in order to live healthy lives. My inspiration came from my love for the man in my life, who realized — and helped me to realize — that no piece of meat or slice of pizza will ever be more important than the love we have for our family. After all, that's what gives our lives real meaning. We never know how long our lives will last, but we can make whatever years or moments we have the very best they can be. Les and I learned that improving our health is truly an act of love, and that without good health, nothing else matters.

Apply this lesson to your own life. To win any personal tug-of-war, ask yourself: "What is really most important?" If you are deeply and com-

pletely honest, the obvious conclusion you achieve may not only surprise you, but can provide you with tools to last a lifetime.

In the years following Les' angioplasty, I continued to learn as much as
possible about healthy eating, and began the process of transforming
myself into a health-conscious cook. I was not previously a gourmet cook
or even a mother who particularly enjoyed preparing meals. I was, however, a teacher, and decided to use that experience to its best advantage.

Realizing that this journey would be lifelong, I continued to experiment
with, and create, many healthy and tasty dishes for my husband (who,
by the way, could easily win an award for raising the art of finicky eating
to new levels). Our process of trial and learning has led us to understand
that healthy eating does not have to mean boring, flavorless eating. It
simply means applying certain modifications. In the process you will
come to realize that you absolutely *can* turn your own particular vice...
"versa".

CHAPTER SIX:
CHANGE IN COURSE

We would all naturally like to anticipate a full life span. Of course, to justify such an expectation, the concept of "health" must be figured into the equation. As with most everything else in our lives, however, we can only expect to *take out* what we ourselves *put in*. Many of us take good health for granted until we are touched by what I call "The Big Scare"! Often, it is only when facing a serious illness that we are truly able to begin accepting our mortality, and understand all that goes into living a healthy life.

...Now, all of a sudden, everything had become real... this was happening to me, and it truly felt like only me. Even in the midst of my loving family, I felt stunned, numb, and all alone.

Our lives were once again moving along with what most people would consider normality. Les was nearing a five-year milestone of good follow-up exams, and was back in "well-built" physical condition. Everyone was healthy, happy and on their way, and I was about halfway through the writing of this book. Les and I had just returned from a wonderful trip to Alaska. And then, one evening in September of 1996, I felt a lump in my breast. To this day, I don't know what led my hand there. To be perfectly honest, I was conscientious about getting my yearly mammograms and check-ups, but I had never really bothered with breast self-exams.

I just stepped out of the shower, and for some unexplained instinctive reason, reached for the exact spot where the lump was located. It was as if something told me it was there. Yet, I first "brushed it off" as being nothing, reassuring myself that I was only 41, in excellent health, and that my yearly mammograms had always been normal. But from somewhere deep inside, a little voice of concern had me call it to Les' attention.

Les had some limited medical knowledge, and was disturbed after feeling the size, shape and firmness of the lump. I coincidentally had an appointment with my gynecologist, Gary Donovitz, during the following week. But Les felt it was urgent, and following an immediate call to Dr. Donovitz, my appointment was moved up to the very next morning.

After an immediate mammogram and sonogram, I was referred to a surgeon, and a surgical biopsy was performed. As I recovered from the procedure and the anesthesia began to wear off, the doctor informed us that the tumor was malignant... BREAST CANCER! At first, the words did not ring true to my ears. Surely, the doctor was talking about someone else... but the unavoidable expression on Les' face couldn't help but drive the impact of the diagnosis home. It wasn't until later that the reality began to sink in. Although Les was with me every minute, I was overwhelmed with fear, and engulfed in sadness. My fear, my pain, and my tears came in abundance that afternoon, and I was caught in the middle of it all.

This diagnosis seemed especially hard to fathom, because, since Les' problem had come to light, I became quite a crusader, teaching and promoting health through diet, exercise, and lifestyle change. I was delivering corporate seminars across the country to train people in the area of wellness. I had become an expert in response to my husband's own personal experience, and enjoyed sharing that knowledge with many others. I practiced what I preached, and was loving my career as a healthy-lifestyle consultant.

In truth, however, even though my "crusade" was inspired by Les' brush with *his* mortality, somehow, it still was a tale about someone other than myself. Now, all of a sudden, everything had become real... this *was* happening to me, and it truly felt like *only* me. Even in the midst of my loving family, I felt stunned, numb, and all alone.

I hope you will never know the mixed emotions that can accompany a cancer diagnosis. How could I have such a serious illness and feel so healthy at the same time? And how could I presume to teach others how to stay healthy, when I hadn't even managed to stay healthy myself? Beyond the fear that came with the disease, I felt disillusioned, as if everything I stood for had become a sham, and I, a charlatan. It was almost ironic. It seemed that the very beliefs I held so dear had become empty words. I felt my optimism regarding good health quickly slipping away. Among many other things in my life, the writing of this book was placed on the back burner. I now had the job of getting well.

Hard Realities

At the time I was diagnosed, statistics stated that one in every nine women would be diagnosed with breast cancer. As I learned more about this disease, I felt like a victim who did not understand her perpetrator. The cancer seemed like an ugly monster which had invaded my life, and I realized that even making all the "right" choices could not guarantee that I would live cancer-free. There was no history of breast cancer in our family, and I was quite young to have a pre-menopausal malignancy. I had nursed my two children, maintained an appropriate body weight my entire life, and had regular mammograms and yearly check-ups. I had not done regular self-exams, because I thought that since I was conscientious in the other areas of my life, my risk factors for breast cancer were lowered. How wrong I was.

Like many other women, I always heard that regular mammograms can detect cancer, but I had lived as if that meant they *prevented* cancer! Finding that lump opened my eyes to the value of the "early detection" we hear so much about. The truth is, since there is currently no cure for breast cancer, the screening and self-exams leading to early detection only offer improved odds of survival through earlier treatment.

Finding out I had breast cancer was among the worst news that I had ever received. Later, I realized that whether it was providence, Divine Intervention, or just plain luck that led me to check myself at that time, finding the growth had in fact saved my life, or certainly extended it. The lack of knowledge would very likely have been fatal. Indeed, I was remarkably fortunate to have caught this when I did, and am now grateful. Early discovery was once again proven as the first line of defense for survival.

So here I was, trying to face the fact that since age 40, my husband was living with heart disease and now I, at age 41, had breast cancer. Why had fate dealt us these difficult cards?

Following The Path Of Pathology

The cancer was on the borderline between "stage one" and "stage two". I was eventually able to glean from Les that the pathology was actually much worse than I had initially understood. It was very aggressive, and the mitosis (cell division) was alarmingly rapid. The cancer had already eaten its way into the vascular system, and was circulating throughout my body in the bloodstream. The tumor itself was considered a "grade three", the worst of its kind. The only factor of luck in my favor was that all lymph nodes were still clear.

Like a puzzle, many pieces had to fit together. Les managed to find the inside word on the best choices of physicians. He spent day and night researching everything possible about the most effective chemotherapy for this type of cancer, in order to know that I would be receiving the best regimen. Immediate treatment had to be our first focus.

I grew deeply afraid with each passing day. Where had this happy, healthy person gone? What would be left of me, after all that was necessary in the attempt to eradicate this disease? It was now October 1996 (which, coincidentally, is National Breast Cancer Awareness month). One day, while I was watching a TV special featuring interviews with other cancer patients, a young television producer articulated my own feelings. When questioned whether she thought she would live a long life, she smiled and answered: "No." When asked why, she responded: "Because I feel that my own body betrayed me. I don't trust my body anymore."

I too, felt as though my young womanhood had betrayed me.

Is Anybody Listening?

I received a phone call from Kathy Bailey, a professional therapist and dear friend of mine. She communicated a sense of compassion and determination to help me overcome my fear of the illness, and my grief over having this forced upon me. I knew that she specialized in working with cancer patients, but never dreamed that I would be one of those patients, searching desperately for direction.

Soon after entering my new "world of illness", I was contacted by another good friend, Rabbi Liza Stern. Sensing my despair, Liza offered powerful words of hope. She suggested that I notice G-d's presence, even in the midst of my pain. I had always considered myself a devoted and spiritual Jewish woman. However, during the early onset of this illness, I somehow felt separated from G-d. After all, if G-d loved and protected me, why would I have this disease?

After reading Rabbi Harold Kushner's book, *When Bad Things Happen To Good People*, I was somewhat able to accept the diagnosis, but still struggled a great deal with my own spirituality and healing. Another friend, Lynda Friedensohn, advised me not to give the cancer so much power. This dreadful disease had only been a part of my life for two months, yet I was allowing it to overshadow the value of my life's blessings for over 40 years. Still, I wasn't near ready to call this "just a major bump in the road". I didn't understand my friend's words at that time, but with constant love and devotion from my wonderful husband Les and my entire family and friends, it became apparent. I was able to push through my despair until finally I began to feel the warming light of hope. Everyone in my life held on to a clear vision of who I was. When I was unable to recognize myself, there were always loving hands of healing reaching for me. The grip of disease slowly began to release its stranglehold, and I started to believe that I could survive. It was then clear that *my loved ones* were all truly *G-d's presence* at work in my life. Through this closeness, I knew that I had not been, and would never be, abandoned.

Healing Together — Emergence From The Shadow

M y loving sister, Gayle Kamen-Weinstein, guided me in the process of recovery with her support, and suggested the use of healing tapes and meditation. She encouraged me to keep a personal journal as a place for release and celebration, and reminded me of the person I once was. As the student is ready, the teacher will appear. And that teacher was my family, teaching me how to mend from my illness, and loving me through each step of the way.

As time passed, I felt more committed to regaining my healthy mental outlook. With the help of my dear friend Wendy Geisler, I implemented the stress-relieving techniques that I previously taught. Les showed me the value of taking one day at a time, and slowly letting go of the grief that was understandably part of the process. My young children became my encouragement for greeting each new day. I started to feel more optimistic in every sense! I visualized beautiful places to which I had traveled, remembered wonderful days spent with loved ones, and soon recalled, once again, the joy of 41 years of health and happiness.

In March of 1997, after six weeks of radiation (which followed the four months of chemotherapy), I was officially termed a "cancer survivor". I felt a great sense of attainment, and yet a strong burden of responsibility. I concluded, as Rabbi Kushner stated: "I am not nearly as frightened as I was yesterday, and am feeling stronger about tomorrow!"

The rekindling of these feelings that were so precious to me solidified my resolve that I wasn't ready for life to end just yet. Knowing I would do whatever it took to live fueled my empowerment to move on. The desire to live a healthy life, doing only those things that nourish and nurture my body, has become as omnipresent to me as breathing itself. I now live with the goal of living well and joyously, and I am grateful for each new day.

My fondest dream is that I continue to experience the value of a rich and healthy life. My most fervent prayer is that I will never lose the courage to live better every day. My struggle with cancer did not end my life. Instead, it truly gave me a new beginning. For this, I feel eternally blessed.

My further hope is that you, dear reader, may find, in the words of Les' and my story, the hunger to seek a happier, healthier life for yourself, and the courage to keep pursuing that life every day.

CHAPTER SEVEN:
RECIPE FOR A WEALTH OF HEALTH...
THE BODY IS THE SOUL'S HOUSE

Wellness is not simply the absence of disease. I have realized the importance of self-mainte-nance and management of my own good health, and have accepted it as if it were another full-time job. With the onset of managed care over the past decade, much has been said about the prevention of illness, in-cluding information about risk factors, and step-by-step do's and don'ts for good health. We must first realize that maintaining our well-being is ultimately up to us. But what's a person to do? Staying well is not quite as simple as following the old cliché, "An apple a day keeps the doctor away." Understanding and applying our knowl-edge requires work, honesty, work, commitment, work, and more work. Is it worth it? The answer is a resound-ing *yes*... because it's all that we have. It's living.

Understanding and applying our knowledge requires work, honesty, work, commitment, work, and more work. Is it worth it? The answer is a resounding yes... because it's all that we have.

If we are struck with an illness, we are usually guided and supported by a medical team of trained profession-als, from diagnosis through treatment. To continue on a healthy track afterward, however, can be both challeng-ing and frightening. Considering the other option, you would think that most people would certainly choose to work toward optimal recovery. But many, perhaps most, people really don't know how.

We have, in fact, become a society that needs to be re-taught how to eat, how to sleep, and yes, how to live. All of this requires change, of course. Whatever your own reason for making that change, I'm certain it springs from the desire that most of us share: to live a long and healthy life. But perhaps you're having trouble getting started. Well, maybe I can help.

I suggest that there are four basic elements to any lifestyle change.

1. First, and of utmost importance, *don't merely accept, but also desire the change and the life-enhancing benefits that it has to offer.* You must *want* to live longer and healthier before you can make any turn onto a better road. For some of us, including Les and me, it's as if we have been given a second chance. A deep, earnest desire will also give you the power to want to…

2. *Learn how to* **incorporate the change.** Your desire will further fuel you with the ability to always remain focused on what you actually…

3. *Enjoy!* Yes, the change can, and should, ultimately be joyful. (Later, we will spell out some examples of actual ways you can program your mind.) And finally, you must…

4. *Adopt your new and improved path as a true, integral and naturally permanent part of your very being.* Let it become as simple and routine as brushing your teeth. Remember: you are doing it for yourself as well as for the ones you love.

Feel the change, think the change and make the change, allowing reasonable time and patience during the transition. Above all, genuinely *enjoy the change every day* on two levels. First, because everything about your new lifestyle really does feel better, both physically and psychologically. Second, because the real priorities in your life will be easier to envision and attain. As you hold fast to the vision of *your purpose* in life, the images motivating you will seem to materialize.

Of one thing I am certain: *Do not take good health for granted.* On the other hand, don't become too obsessed with the concept of "perfect" health. As a matter of fact, these days it is really quite rare to find perfect health throughout most families. Which leads me again to the point that health is definitely a family matter. Even if you are convinced that you are already in perfect health and need to do nothing further, making good food choices daily should at least be considered an obligation to set a good example for your children.

L es and I found it quite interesting that there are numerous similarities in the recommended diets for the care and prevention of both heart disease and cancer. A regular healthy diet is an invaluable tool for stacking your odds against a myriad of diseases. First, however, you must open your eyes and rid yourself of the "it-won't-happen-to-me" syndrome.

Some of us do not make healthy choices because we lack the necessary information needed to do so. But another significant reason many of us have poor diets or unhealthy lifestyles is, simply, denial! We hear the health hype and see daily evidence of illness, but convince ourselves that it affects only others and surely not us… at least until it is "up close and personal". In reality, our blood pressure may be elevated, or our heart vessels clogged, without our even knowing. Just ask Les.

Many people use denial as a way to disguise fear. We are all ultimately afraid of poor health. Fear can paralyze our motivation and intention. But note that within the word "fear" is the word "ear". Talking about what we fear, as well as listening to others, can ease and relieve fear, allowing movement to take place. When we accept our own mortality, we can take more control of our destiny. Why is it so simple and yet so hard? A simple walk, a red apple, a glass of water… why does the commitment to incorporate these things into our daily life seem so difficult?

In reality, it is not all that difficult. As Les and I discovered, a great place to start improving your lifestyle is in your daily food selections. In the course of one day, each of us makes as many as 12 to 15 food choices.

That can conceivably be over 100 selections per week.

Sending your body the kinds of foods that make digestion easy, while keeping your stomach satisfied, is a daily challenge, but it is well worth accomplishing. Choosing proper foods is at least as essential as knowing what keys to press to access storage of files in a computer.

I invite you to pick up this cookbook as a jump-start to maintain or regain good health. Small steps can lead to huge results. Using positive mind control to "stick with it" always proves worthwhile. I urge you to use the recipes in this book as learning tools to cook and eat in a way in which your body can successfully do its intended job. You may just gain even more in personal knowledge than you lose in pounds.

What you will find in the following chapters is a "road map", made up of the information needed to plan a healthier lifestyle. I'll also share many of the recipes we've tried, tested, and tasted — and found to be absolutely delicious. I hope you find the information useful, and the dishes as delectable as your (longer) life promises to be.

CHAPTER EIGHT:
GETTING TO THE HEART OF WHAT MATTERS

Each day, most of us are in a race against time to cook, eat, accomplish our tasks, and feel good. We sometimes even think of vices such as alcohol, smoking, and the abuse of food as being "perks" that make us feel good. This is particularly evident when we become trapped in the misconception that the satisfying feelings resulting from food equate to gratification. Even worse, we tend to justify these false rewards by convincing ourselves that we deserve dividends for our hard work.

...we are literally harming ourselves and those we love, in the name of artificial fulfillment.

Sadly, these habits are usually short-lived, ineffective attempts to fill the empty spaces in our lives. Believe it or not, it has also been found that for certain underlying reasons, some people are living out a hidden desire to inflict subtle punishment upon themselves or those around them. Either way, we are literally harming ourselves and those we love, in the name of artificial fulfillment. Often, the true subconscious motive goes unknown. In any event, finding a way to recognize and come to terms with our mental and emotional state gives us substantial advantages in the pursuit to gain more control over our lives.

As we go through life, we are faced with many choices. The most difficult are those that require us to exercise some form of personal control. Whether we are struggling to give up nicotine, shed pounds, or begin our commitment to eating well, it can feel like being on a roller-coaster ride, making bumpy stops at unscheduled stations. Sometimes we stay on faultlessly, and other times, holding on seems difficult. It is important to realize that an occasional stumble off the track *does not mean you've failed*. More fairly, view such occurrences as small side-steps that you can easily correct to get back on track. Just as you consciously gave yourself permission to deviate from your new, improved style, you can also choose to return to it. As long as you don't misuse the concept of "human imperfection" as an excuse for straying, you won't waste your time and energy wallowing in guilt. Instead, you will emerge from the experience with just a little more wisdom, perhaps even a renewed commitment and a "refueled" strength of purpose.

You are not alone in feeling that feeding yourself and your family in a healthy manner can be a challenge. Even without the media's constant barrage of invitations to savor the delights of this or that rich, fat-filled offering, you are still faced with the sheer inertia of your own experiences. It can be very difficult to change something you've been doing — and enjoying — all your life, even if you know it is harmful. Understandably, new behaviors must usually offer some reward or personal incentive to continue. I hope you will use the recipes in this book to get the immediate gratification you crave, while abiding by your commitment to health. I invite you to incorporate these heart-healthy recipes into your hectic life and experience the genuine nourishment that these morsels offer your soul as well as your body.

It is our desire that this book will help bring to light how cooking and eating properly can offer a lifetime of delicious repasts. By using these techniques and recipes throughout the year, including (or I should say, *especially!*) on holidays and special occasions, you will find that what initially seemed to be a rigid discipline can ultimately become a delightful way of life.

With the help of this information, I encourage you to turn this challenge

Recipes For The Heart, Morsels For The Soul

into a priority that becomes a key focus in your life. Rather than viewing healthy eating as hard work and sacrifice, give yourself praise for the gift of well-being that you are giving to your loved ones and your own body. Permit yourself to truly enjoy the satisfaction that comes from healthy eating, and notice how much better it feels… physically and psychologically. Use the recipes in this book as rewards you give yourself in your newly chosen lifestyle — a lifestyle devoted to gaining added years of joyous, healthy living.

One thing to keep in mind: Don't jump in so abruptly that you completely throw out your family favorites, or you might be on the road Monday and off again by Friday. "Cold turkey" may be delicious, but it's not the best way to change your family's eating habits. Start by incorporating these recipes into familiar meals, and begin to purchase products that can substantially trim the fat content from most everything you eat. Carefully scrutinize oils, butter and margarine, sauces, and dairy. Keep your eagle eye especially tuned for indications that these and other fat-bearing products may be secondary ingredients of other foods.

Try starting with these healthier replacements:

ITEM	REPLACE WITH
Butter	Vegetable or Fat-Free Butter Spray
Eggs	Egg Substitute or Egg Whites (2 whole eggs =1/2 cup cholesterol-free egg substitute or 4 egg whites)
Cheese	Fat-Free or Reduced-Fat Cheese (such as Ricotta)
Hot Dogs	Fat-Free Hot Dogs or Turkey Dogs
Cream Cheese	Fat-Free or Reduced-Fat Cream Cheese Spread
Sour Cream	Fat-Free (or at least Light if necessary) Cream Cheese or Fat-Free Plain Yogurt Mixed with Lemon Juice

ITEM	REPLACE WITH
Nuts	Grape Nuts Cereal
Chocolate	Fat-Free Hot Fudge or Cocoa or Carob
Mayonnaise	Fat-Free Mayonnaise or Mustard
Basting w/Butter	Non-Fat Broth, Fat-Free Butter or Oil Sprays, Fruit Juice, or Water
Butter Bread Crumbs	Crushed Cereals, Dried, Baked or Toasted Bread Crumbs from Sourdough or Whole-Grain Breads

We'll discuss fat and other facts of nutritional life in the chapters to follow. But first, let's take a detour through the supermarket so you can get started on building the perfect pantry for your new lifestyle.

CHAPTER NINE:
SUPER MARKETING AND LABEL-EASE

The typical American family kitchen is traditionally stocked with high-fat, high-calorie foods, and is very lean on whole grains and fresh foods. Keeping fresh fruits and veggies well stocked should be a priority for healthy living. Create a well-balanced kitchen with fresh fruits and vegetables, nonfat dairy, only the leanest types of meats (such as turkey-breast products), seafood, egg substitutes, rice, beans, whole grain breads, pasta, nonfat vegetable cooking spray, and nonfat butter substitutes.

Keeping fresh fruits and veggies well stocked should be a priority for healthy living.

Creating the perfect pantry requires a four-step process:

1. Take an inventory of the products you currently have in stock.

2. Arrange these items according to categories — such as cereals, snacks, sauces, condiments, baking items, canned goods, spices, and seasonings.

3. Create a grocery list of low-fat or no-fat "switch" items that you will store in your new *healthy eating* pantry. Having these items readily available will allow for greater efficiency while planning for, and preparing, your low-fat meals.

4. Experiment with different brands of low-fat items, because the taste, texture and degree of moisture can vary with different brands. Manu-

facturers are coming out with new items every day, and the list changes often. Once you have discovered an enjoyable brand of a particular item, make it a regular part of your kitchen stock. Make modifications slowly, in stages, so that this change will become a permanent one that your entire family will enjoy. For example, shift from regular mayonnaise to light or low-fat (for as short a duration as possible), and then move on to completely nonfat mayonnaise. It is often very tasty to combine fat-free and low-fat mixtures of certain ingredients until everyone develops their gradual change in taste.

Watching Your Budget While You Watch Your Health

The average American family spends between $6,000 and $8,000 each year on groceries. You may have already noticed that low-fat does not necessarily mean low price. There are, however, ways to keep your low-fat budget "lean".

Stocking up on fruits and veggies will trim your waist and your budget. You can buy two dozen oranges for the cost of one container of chocolate-chip ice cream. Buying foods for a healthy diet (even if you pick very exotic fruits and gourmet pastas) costs about seventy-five cents per person *less* per day than shopping for the typical high-fat diet. According to a study by the Basset Research Institute at Cooperstown, New York and the Department of Nutrition at Pennsylvania State University, a family of four following this tip for their healthier diet may well realize a savings of $1,095 per year.

Since you are beginning to make lifestyle changes, you will also be monitoring portion control much more closely. Many of your more expensive items will stretch further, due to the streamlining of portions. Whenever you are preparing recipes, try to "Power Cook". Make many more servings than the recipe calls for, split the item up into smaller portions, and freeze the extras for another meal.

> Never give up in your quest for the healthier versions of the products you like. The grocery-store market is a very competitive business, and managers will do all that they can to keep their customers coming back. If you do not see a certain product you want, ask the manager to order it and call you when it comes in.

Many companies sell and distribute new items through test-market cities and may not distribute all of their items throughout the country. Entenmann's is a good example of this distribution policy. If you find a product in another city, you can always call the 800 phone number and ask for current availability information in your city (or you can stock up and ship home).

"Meal plan" by deciding on your entrees for the week, and develop your weekly shopping list. Take your list and try not to grocery shop when you are hungry. In that physical and mental state, everything looks good and has taste appeal, sometimes causing temptation and possibly a slight difficulty in maintaining control. Stick to your list and allow enough time to read labels, monitor unplanned purchases carefully, and explore all the new products.

> Major trends continue to occur in the supermarket environment. Many of the items are now fast *and* fresh. For instance, many of the pastas are fresh, but require refrigeration and do not have a long shelf life. Some low-fat and nonfat items do not have as many preservatives or additives, and therefore have a shorter shelf life than traditional processed foods. So always check the shelf life date, and note on the package whether refrigeration is needed. Also read labels carefully, as not all "low-fat" and "no-fat" foods really live up to the name. And remember to check the serving size!

Read The Label
For Setting A Healthier Table

Since the FDA has standardized the labeling of products, all products must now include a four-part label:

1. "Serving size" is one of the most useful pieces of information. Serving sizes must be consistent with standards of the industry, allowing you to make choices comparing one product to another. All of the nutrition information will be based on "serving size".

2. "Calories" and "calories from fat" will include a total number of calories in each serving size, and how much of those calories are coming from fat. After considering the recommended servings per day from each group from the Food Pyramid (which we'll explore later in this chapter), be sure to determine how many calories you are consuming by eating more than one serving size. If the number of calories coming from fat is high, then the product you are eating probably has a high fat-gram count.

3. "Nutrients" listed are total fat, saturated fat (two extremely important areas on which to focus; see Chapter 11 for more information), cholesterol, sodium, carbohydrates (listed as a total of simple and complex), fiber, vitamins A and C, calcium, and iron.

4. "Daily values for nutrients" tells you the nutritional value each product has and how it falls into nutritional requirements for a 2000-calorie diet and a 2500-calorie diet. At the very bottom of the label are the daily values. These recommendations are based on minimum and maximum daily requirements needed to consume if you are on a 2000-calorie diet. If you are consuming more or less than 2000 calories per day, you will have to adjust your requirements.

Zero Means Nothing, And That Means A Lot

Marketing can sometimes be misleading. Take a look at the way in which products have been defined, and you'll realize the importance of understanding labels:

MARKETING CLAIM (per serving)	TRANSLATION
Fat-Free	½ gram or less
Low-Fat	Up to 3 grams of fat
Extra Lean	Up to 5 grams of fat
Lean	Up to 10 grams of fat
Low Calorie	Up to 40 calories
Light	Can refer to texture or color of food, and not necessarily to the fat or calorie content

What is Healthy, Anyway? (Secrets Of The Great Food Pyramid)

Many people mistakenly believe that eating healthy means going hungry, depriving themselves of their favorites, and limiting their food selections. Thankfully, this is not the case. To change our eating habits, however, we must first have a model or standard to work from, and some clearly defined goals to work toward.

Since the government often tends to become involved in the well-being of its citizens, I thought it seemed logical that there would be some form of "clearinghouse" for the information I was seeking. And I was right. In cooperation with medical researchers in the private sector, the United States Department of Agriculture has developed what it calls the Food Guide Pyramid as a model for healthy eating.

The Food Guide Pyramid is an easy, workable guide for balancing variety and nutrition. It replaces the old basic "Four Food Groups" model (which many of us studied in school). There are now six food groups. The emphasis is on balance, variety, and portion size, with moderation being the key. Whenever I teach heart-healthy eating, I like to keep the instructions simple and easy to understand and use. The Food Guide Pyramid is a wonderful tool to help achieve that goal.

On the following pages, I will present the pyramid itself (see Figure 9-1), along with a plain-language description of what it all means.

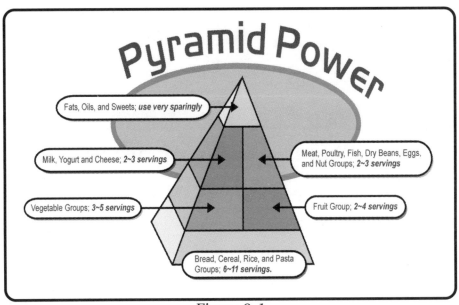

Figure 9-1

By the pyramid's shape, note that the lower levels equate to higher recommended serving volumes. The base, or foundation, of the pyramid includes grains, breads, cereal, rice, and pasta. The next level up is comprised of fruits and vegetables, and the next, even narrower level, consists of modest amounts of dairy products, meats, and other high-protein foods. At the very peak, we find fats, oils, and sweets. This section comes to a very sharp point creating the top — and narrowest — portion of the pyramid. Notice that in this area, no recommended serving sizes are given. The only instruction, however, is to *use sparingly*.

The descriptions of recommended servings can be somewhat confusing and difficult to translate into everyday eating habits. Just remember that each section represents a food category, and, with the exception of the top portion of the pyramid, indicates a range for the recommended number of servings to be consumed daily. And to further guide you, here, in another form, are the USDA's Food Guide Pyramid daily-serving recommendations:

Bread, Cereal, Rice, and Pasta	6~11 servings per day
Vegetables	3~5 servings per day
Fruits	2~4 servings per day
Milk, Yogurt, and Cheese	2~3 servings per day
Meat, Poultry, Fish, Beans, Eggs, and Nuts	2~3 servings per day
Fats, Oils, and Sweets	Use Sparingly

So, what actually makes up one serving? Naturally, we all have highly individual appetites, so our personal interpretations of what constitutes "a serving" may vary widely. Les, for example, is five feet, five inches tall, and was never heavy. One would think that it wouldn't take much to fill him up. Quite the opposite is true — something that always elicited amazement in those who ate with us. When everybody else (including the really big guys) pushed away from the table, groaning, Les would still be wading into his meal as if he hadn't eaten in days. His concept of what constituted a portion was obviously quite different from that of most people. To get an idea of what the nutritionists consider a serving to be, see the chart on the following page.

Some common examples of food categories and typical servings are:

CATEGORY:	TYPICAL SINGLE SERVING:
Grains	1 cup dry cereal; ½ cup dense cereal; ½ cup cooked cereal; 1 slice of bread or ½ a bagel; 4 crackers; 2 (2.5 oz.) waffles; 3 small pancakes; ½ cup cooked rice or pasta
Fruits	1 piece fresh fruit; ½ cup chopped fruit; ¾ cup fruit juice
Vegetables	½ cup chopped vegetables; 1 cup leafy greens; ¾ cup vegetable juice
Meats	2~3 ounces cooked lean meat; poultry, seafood, beef or pork; 1 low-fat hot dog; ½ cup dried beans (cooked); ½ cup nuts
Dairy Products	1 cup milk; 1 cup yogurt or frozen yogurt; 1 slice cheese; ½ cup cottage cheese, 1 egg; ¼ cup egg substitute

If you're still confused about serving sizes, here's another "thumbnail" aid to approximating quantity, based upon an average adult:

Your fist equals:	About 1 cup or 1 medium whole fruit
Your thumb equals:	About 1 ounce cheese or meat
Your thumb tip equals:	About 1 tablespoon
Your fingertip equals:	About 1 teaspoon
Your palm equals:	About 3 ounces cooked meat, poultry or fish

As with anything else, when something works, it catches on, spurring a host of imitations. Since the original food guide pyramid, there have been others that sprouted up, including a vegetarian pyramid, and various ethnic versions. And that's fine by me; this is one "pyramid scheme" from which we can all benefit!

CHAPTER TEN:
THE MEAT OF THE SUBJECT... THE MORE WE KNOW, THE MORE WE CAN CONTROL

o really get started with healthy eating habits, it's important to know some basic facts about nutrition. You may have learned — and forgotten — about the essential nutrients back in your high school health class. Or maybe you had a big weekend and slept through class that day. Not to worry: in this chapter, we'll review the nutrients, as well as some other important elements in the foods we eat. So if you promise to stay awake for the next few pages, I promise to keep it relatively brief (and there won't be a test afterwards)!

...The significant factor to consider isn't just the number of calories you take in, but the source and ratio of those calories compared to the number you "burn".

Calories Count

Calories, typically regarded as the annoyance of dieters, are, in actuality, units of energy in the form of heat. Once converted into a useful state, they perform many functions in our bodies, such as aiding in digestion, and helping provide energy for all of our physical activities, including breathing and heart function. However, when you consume more calories than you need, you gain weight, and when you eat fewer calories than you require, you lose weight. The significant factor to consider isn't just the number of calories you take in, but the source and ratio of those calories compared to the number you "burn" during the course of your normal activities.

Carbohydrates... It's Simple: Eat Complex

There has been a trend, of late, to view carbohydrates as the enemies of a healthy diet. Unfortunately, this trend has found its voice in a number of celebrities, whose credibility is founded more in good publicity than in medical knowledge. Contrary to many of these claims, the body needs carbohydrates to run at top efficiency. Made up of sugars and starches that our body can easily break down into fuel for energy, carbohydrates for the body might be analogized to premium gasoline for a car.

Carbohydrates are broken down into two categories: simple and complex. Simple carbohydrates are tiny molecules of sugar found in such foods as honey, table sugar, and baked goods or sweets. These carbohydrates are composed of groups of simple sugars fused together, forming a long molecular chain. Complex carbohydrates, also known as starches, supply the body with a hearty stock of energy. They also team up with protein to fight infection, and help our skin and bones.

By the way, some fruits and vegetables have both carbohydrates and proteins. Do you know which ones? Well, I won't keep you in suspense. Here's a short list:

♥ Asparagus
♥ Cauliflower
♥ Potato
♥ Sweet Potato
♥ Sweet Corn

Carbohydrates start to digest almost as soon as they mix with saliva. Found in vegetables, fruits, beans, and grains, complex carbohydrates supply the body with a much more long-lasting source of energy than do simple carbohydrates. Complex carbohydrates cause the blood sugar to rise and fall gradually at a steady rate, allowing sugar levels to be maintained over a one- to three-hour period. Think of them as time-release calories which are dispensed throughout your body as they are needed, as opposed to the temporary "rush" of energy you get from the simple carbohydrates — i.e., the sugars — commonly found in most candy, sodas, and other sweet treats.

Pasta and potatoes are among the foods that contain complex carbohydrates. However, they also carry high calories as a result of their weight. Eating excessive amounts of foods that are heavy in carbohydrates (even complex) can easily turn into extra pounds when you give your body little or no exercise to burn them off. Common toppings, such as regular margarine or butter and cheese, can contribute a lot of unnecessary and potentially dangerous fat as well. Here again is where we learn to acquire tastes for nonfat substitutes. For example, salsa or fat-free Ranch dressing can be delicious over a baked potato. When you need energy, pastas are a food of choice.

Fruits And Vegetables... "When More is Less"

Can enough ever be said about this food group? Vegetables and fruits are the "dietary heroes" of any health plan. As stated by the National Cancer Institute, eating five fruits and five vegetables a day is one of the most important choices we can make to help promote good health and prevention of disease. Fruits and veggies are a terrific mixture of complex carbohydrates, and they come in high on vitamins A and C and low on calories. Most of these gems are almost completely fat-free, are made of up natural sugars, and are rich in fiber and beta-carotene. Additionally, there has been a lot of hype regarding the benefits of natural juices from fruits and vegetables, and their ability to help maintain a resistance against many major diseases. There have even been a number of companies offering concentrated capsules or tablets for the purpose of supplementing a variety of vegetable and fruit extracts and the accompanying phyto-nutrients.

While the jury's still out on some of these supplements, there's enough information on the benefits of fresh fruits and veggies, as well as the juices from same, to be convincing that they truly belong in a healthy diet. So, whenever the urge for a soda strikes, try a nice, delicious, refreshing glass of 100% real juice! You should be able to find a variety in almost any convenient store. And when your sweet tooth acts up, don't reach for a candy bar. Instead, choose high-fiber, unprocessed carbohydrates such as apples or bananas (we'll have more on fiber in just a little while).

I hope you agree by now that these members of the food pyramid really do a body good. But how do you know which ones are the best? Well, Mother Nature does not do anything by accident. Color is usually a good clue that a particular fruit or vegetable is packing a potent nutritional punch! A good many of the healthy ones are meant to attract attention with their bright colors.

Wherever your own preferences lead you, it's worth repeating: a diet rich in fruits and veggies can cut down on risk of colds, flu, and many cancers. Less illness means less stress, less medication, and fewer doctor visits. So grab your sweet potatoes and oranges, and go for the gold!

Protein Power

Protein is the body's repairman and "jack of all trades". Found in every cell, protein helps to build and repair almost everything in our bodies. Proteins are digested gradually, resulting in a slow rise and fall in blood sugar levels, lasting between three and five hours. Good food sources should have at least 25 grams of protein per serving.

What are the best, and healthiest, sources of protein? Some scientists now believe that a mixture of both animal and plant proteins are essential for the body. However, you need to choose your protein sources wisely. For example, the amount of protein in a single portion of beans and rice is equivalent to that in a moderate size T-bone steak; both have 22 grams.

But a four-ounce T-bone has 24 grams of saturated fat, while a 1¼ cup serving of rice and beans has *less than half a gram* of fat. Obviously, there are dramatic differences!

Poultry

L oaded with protein, poultry is lower in total fat and unsaturated fat than most red meats. Remember to use white-meat poultry and trim the skin and fat. Poultry is extremely easy to prepare. It is also a good source of iron. Both turkey and chicken can be prepared by baking, broiling, and other methods that promote low-fat results. One three-ounce serving of skinless roasted white turkey meat has 133 calories and 2.7 grams of total fat, less than one gram of which is saturated fat. So eat up. Stay lean and mean about your effort to eat poultry in place of red meats. Larger, older birds such as roosters are fattier. Smaller, younger birds are leaner and should be your first choice. Ducks and geese are high in saturated fat. Remember to stay strictly with the white-meat sections.

Some Meaty Advice

I promote cutting out red meat from your diet, but if you feel you have to eat red meat, by all means, check your numbers — calories, fat grams, etc. I'm including a chart in this section to give you some examples. *But please note that all of these totals are based on a trimmed three-ounce piece of meat after cooking.* In other words, a very small piece, often compared to the size of an audio cassette tape. (Remember, we're saying *audio*, not *video!*) Processed meats should contain no more than three grams of fat per ounce. Be aware, however, that, as mentioned earlier, many processed meats are high in sodium. Organ meats are very high in cholesterol and should be avoided. On the following page are some more tips on buying and handling meat.

♥ When buying lamb, look for the meat that is pink or dark red. The leanest part of the lamb is the leg.

♥ If you really enjoy veal, look for a light pink appearance. The leanest cuts of veal are the leg cutlet, arm steak, rib chop, and top round.

♥ When using any red meat, always trim visible fat and discard.

♥ Take steps to avoid food-borne illness! First, be sure that all meat you buy is fresh, and if you are defrosting, thaw it in the refrigerator, not on the kitchen counter. Always wash knives and cutting boards often, and keep them clean.

♥ Be very aware that the labeling on meats is different than on most other foods. Percentage fat labels on all meat products are by weight and not by calories. For example, some turkey bologna labels claim they are 80% fat-free. The 20% fat that is noted on this claim is 20% of the *weight*, not the *calories*. When calculating the percentage of calories from fat, realize that an 80% fat-free item actually derives 72% of its calories from fat. If you must have an occasional meat "fix", make wise choices by looking for lean meats that are labeled as being at least 96% fat free.

Now here is that chart I promised you, containing some general information on a few common cuts of meat:

LEAN CUT MEATS	CALORIES	TOTAL FAT	SATURATED FAT
Beef:			
Eye Of Round	140	4 grams	2 grams
Top Round	150	4 grams	1 gram
Tip Round	160	6 grams	2 grams
Tenderloin Steak	180	9 grams	3 grams
Pork:			
Tenderloin	140	4 grams	1 gram
Boneless Ham	125	4 grams	2 grams
Lamb:			
Loin Chop	180	8 grams	3 grams

Water

Like the planet that supports us, our bodies are composed of about three-fourths water. Every tissue and cell in the body has water. Obviously, water is essential to our survival. It is also an important aid in losing weight and keeping it off. Although water contains no calories, it contributes to a feeling of fullness. Many reports indicate that when you sip water along with a meal, there's also a greater chance that you will be satisfied with smaller food portions.

Of course, weight loss / maintenance is just one reason it's important to drink plenty of water. After all, the body uses water for most of its processes, from digestion to sweating. You probably realize how important it is to have extra water when you're exercising, to avoid the dangers of dehydration. And water is essential for maintaining optimal energy levels through the day. In fact, many people who feel lethargic or listless may be suffering more from dehydration than from lack of sleep. To maintain a proper fluid balance, most nutritional experts recommend that you drink at least eight (8-ounce) glasses of water or other fluids each day.

Caffeine

Coffee and cola hounds, beware. Historically subject to debate, caffeine is a drug, long associated with physical and psychological dependency. This drug comes from a family of chemical compounds called xanthines. It is a stimulant and can cause side effects that include insomnia, increased or irregular heartbeat, and nervousness. It may also irritate the stomach, deplete the body's calcium and iron levels, and can contribute to various forms of tumors and cancers. Caffeine offers no nutritional value, but does have the ability to arouse feelings of hunger.

As with any addiction, it is generally advisable to alter your habit by first realizing that you truly can do without it. Find satisfying alternatives, but until you can beat it completely, try to stay within the acceptable limit of 200 milligrams per day. The road map to maintaining wellness should include gradual, comfortable withdrawal, replacing regular coffee and sodas with caffeine-free varieties. Better still, try making the switch to decaffeinated herbal teas or fruit and vegetable juices.

Dietary Fiber

Fiber is a magical dietary element that has no calories, but contributes to a feeling of fullness. It also facilitates the processing of waste in your gastrointestinal tract, and helps prevent constipation and related ills. Adequate fiber intake decreases your chances of contracting colon cancer, since carcinogenic substances don't have as much time to linger and cause damage. And because it removes cholesterol from the small intestines, fiber also benefits your heart.

There are two types of fiber. *Soluble fiber* can absorb water, after which it is transformed into a soft gel. Soluble fiber is found in fruits, oats, legumes, rye, and barley. *Insoluble fiber* does not absorb water. Its sources include whole wheat products, bran, and the skins of vegetables and fruits. Broccoli, onions, sweet potatoes, and apples are some foods that are high in fiber.

Despite all that has been written about fiber in the past couple of decades, most Americans still do not get enough fiber in their diets. It is generally recommended that we consume 20 to 35 grams of fiber per day. This doesn't mean that you should immediately start sprinkling bran on all your food. One slight caveat with fiber is that excessive quantities can also speed the good stuff — particularly essential minerals such as calcium, iron, and zinc — through your body before these nutrients can be absorbed. And too much fiber can irritate your bowel. The good news is that when fiber is consumed through whole foods, such as those fruits, vegetables and grains that play such an important part in the Food Pyramid, you can get enough fiber, and it's almost impossible to get *too* much. It is also felt that whole grains can help reduce the risks of heart disease and cancer. One common marketing message with which I fully agree is that breakfast cereals that are good sources of fiber can be a great way to begin your day!

Foods that are rich in fiber:
- ♥ Plant or roughage foods
- ♥ Seeds, grains, peels, oats, and popcorn
- ♥ Bulk foods such as rice and beans
- ♥ Fresh fruits and vegetables
- ♥ Whole-grain breads, cereals, and crackers

Dairy

Components of dairy products are vital to our growth, and, as we have all heard throughout our childhood, help us develop strong bones and teeth. Dairy products are rich in calcium and vitamin D, and can therefore help prevent osteoporosis, a demineralization and weakening of the bones. This condition is particularly prevalent in women post-menopause, and is a culprit in creating the vulnerability to hip fractures in the elderly.

So how can you add enough dairy to your diet without overdoing it on the fat intake? To begin with, choose from low-fat dairy products such as skim milk. High-calcium, low-fat products can also be substituted in preparing many dishes. For example, substitute evaporated skim milk, which is made with cultured skim milk, for heavy cream or buttermilk. Substitute nonfat (or at least low-fat) cheese. Be aware that cheddar cheese and other hard cheeses are very high in fat. If you cannot go without these cheeses, cut the brick into one-inch square cubes, and try to limit yourself to a maximum of one to three cubes daily. And again, read the labels! Eat only dairy products (including ice creams and dairy creamers) that are low in saturated fat.

MILK: THE DETAILS (based on a 1-cup serving size):		
Type	Calories	Fat
Whole*	159	8.5 grams
2%	145	5.0 grams
1%	102	2.6 grams
Skim	80	0.2 grams
Buttermilk	99	2.0 grams
Goat's milk	168	10 grams
Low-fat evaporated	220	6 grams
*(usually recommended for children under the age of two)		

Cholesterol Conscious?

This famous waxy, yellowish, mashed potato-like substance (sounds tasty, doesn't it?) is produced mostly by the liver. It can be found in various parts of the body, and is actually essential for fat digestion. Our bodies also use cholesterol to form cell membranes and hormones. We produce about two-thirds of the total amount of cholesterol that we need, while the rest comes from our diet. Since cholesterol is present in animal products, it follows that a diet high in animal products (such as meats and dairy) is also high in cholesterol.

The body produces about 1,000 milligrams (mg) of cholesterol each day. A high-fat, high-cholesterol diet adds far too much extra cholesterol to our bloodstream. Although the daily recommended intake level is no more than 200 to 300 milligrams of dietary cholesterol, the average American consumes 400 to 600 milligrams from dietary sources daily — in other words, double what they should be consuming.

Cholesterol is insoluble in water and must be carried in the blood by protein substances called lipoproteins. Lipoproteins are substances composed primarily of fat and protein. Each lipoprotein carries different amounts of cholesterol. Low-density lipoproteins (LDL) carry mostly cholesterol, fats and triglycerides. High levels of LDL have been strongly linked to the development of coronary artery disease.

Another type of carrier, the high-density lipoproteins (HDL), consist mostly of protein. HDL carry cholesterol away from the body cells, and back to the liver to be excreted in the bile. One way to remember the difference between HDL and LDL is to associate the "H" in HDL with "healthy". Conversely, I find that it helps me remember that LDL is an undesirable type of cholesterol by thinking of the "L" in LDL as standing for "lousy". Although experts recommend a total blood cholesterol level below 200 milligrams, the individual levels and ratio between HDL and LDL are usually a more important factor to be considered. It is preferable to have a higher HDL and a low LDL.

As described earlier, saturated fatty acids are the main dietary culprit in elevating blood cholesterol levels. The American Heart Association recommends that you limit your saturated fatty acid intake to less than 10 percent of the total calories taken in each day. You should be aware, however, that not all saturated fats come from animal origins. Foods of plant origin that contain high amounts of saturated fats include "tropical oils", such as coconut oil, palm oil, and cocoa butter. These oils may be cholesterol free, but the saturated fats they contain can raise your LDL levels as easily as a greasy hamburger. A common example of a possible hazard in disguise is liquid coffee creamer that is marketed as "non-dairy", but doesn't claim to be fat-free. Read the nutrition labels, and pay particular attention to the fat count. If you notice any of the above oils, don't walk away; *run* away... or at the very least, *exercise extreme caution* by using these very sparingly!

Remember, LDL deposits itself on the arterial walls, while HDL removes cholesterol from the bloodstream. LDL has a thin layer of protein and tends to accumulate in the blood vessels, while HDL has a thick layer of protein and actually helps eliminate cholesterol from the body. Excess cholesterol or plaque collection on the inner walls of the blood vessels causes the condition known as arteriosclerosis. As these fatty deposits continue to build, they restrict, and can even totally block, the oxygen-rich blood flow through the vessels. When significant narrowing results in the vessels that nourish the heart, the payoff is coronary artery disease, which can be accompanied by chest pain and / or a heart attack. As Les and I (as well as a frightening number of other people) have discovered, this condition can exist without any pain, symptoms or other indication of a potential problem, even in individuals who seem to be in excellent health. It may only take one quick incident to be fatal. In other words, the "big one" could come at any time without warning. But guess what? Every 1% decrease in your level of total blood cholesterol can correlate to a 2% decrease in your risk of having a heart attack!

In many cases, a low-fat, low-cholesterol diet and regular aerobic-type exercise can help lower blood cholesterol levels. The best advice for all of us is to have our cholesterol levels checked regularly, and to eat sensibly. Upon determination by a physician that it is safe and advisable to do so, we should also maintain a regular exercise program.

What About Eggs?

You are likely familiar with some examples of foods that are high in cholesterol, including red meats, organ meats, dairy products (other than skim), and egg yolks. You have undoubtedly heard that eggs are high in cholesterol, but did you know that the egg contains the highest level of cholesterol of any single food item, and that it is *all* within the yolk? The white of the egg contains no cholesterol, and has less than one-third the calories of the yolk.

    1 egg = 65 calories and 274 milligrams of cholesterol
    1 egg white = 17 calories and 0 cholesterol

Egg substitutes may be used without sacrificing flavor. When choosing egg substitute products, use care in checking the shelf-life (expiration date) and the storage method. The labels on the egg substitute packages will delineate the proper volume equivalents to use for each egg required.

> **EGG SUBSTITUTE SCALE**
> 1 Large Egg = 2 Large Egg Whites
> 1 Large Egg = 3 Tablespoons Egg Substitute
> 1 Large Egg White = 2 Tablespoons Egg Substitute

Triglycerides

Triglycerides are found in both animal and vegetable fats. Triglycerides come in all sizes and shapes, but they all have a similar structure: a glycerol molecule with three fatty acids attached. The liver converts excess calories and foods such as sugars into triglycerides, which are then transported to the blood. As such, triglycerides also contribute to the storage of fat. People with high triglyceride levels should avoid foods such as sweets and processed baked goods. In many cases, triglyceride levels can be lowered through a decrease in sugars and an increase in exercise. We'll have more on sugars later on in this chapter.

Speaking of cholesterol, LDLs, and triglycerides, just what are the desired blood levels? Here is a handy chart:

DESIRED LEVELS	
Total Cholesterol	Less than 200
LDL Cholesterol	Less than 130
HDL Cholesterol	45-55
Triglycerides	Less than 120

If your own levels do not fall within the desired limits, your health-care practitioner will advise you on steps you can take to improve them.

What's The Shake-up On Salt?

The average American is *adding* 3,000 to 6,000 milligrams of salt to his or her diet daily, which is comparable to 1½ to 3½ teaspoons per day. A safe and healthy amount would be less than five milligrams per day, or less than ¼ teaspoon. For a better understanding and comparison, bouillon, most canned soups and dried soup mixes may contain up to 1,000 milligrams per serving. Light salt contains ½ the amount of regular table salt.

Table salt is basically sodium chloride, a mineral that our body needs. The function of sodium is to regulate the proper balance of vital fluids and chemicals throughout our system. Sodium is found in nature and is in most of the foods we eat. We all need *some* salt, but we would get enough naturally from the fresh foods we eat. Fresh fruits and vegetables contain only small amounts of sodium. However, highly processed foods, such as frozen entrees or canned soups, contain a great deal of sodium, because it is frequently added in the processing, especially as a preservative and tenderizer. For example, ½ cup of frozen peas has four milligrams of sodium, while ½ cup of canned peas contains a whopping 367 milligrams.

In fact, ¾ of our dietary sodium is hidden in processed and preserved foods. To offer you more examples: One cup of pudding contains 250 milligrams of sodium. Even a can of soda contains 35 milligrams. Beyond table salt, almost all snack food products are a leading source of sodium. It only takes 10 regular potato chips to furnish you with 200 milligrams. Other items that contain sodium are food additives, such as flavor enhancers, preservatives, and marinades. Large amounts of sodium are found in salad dressings and condiments such as ketchup, relishes, pickles, mustard, soy sauce, and, of course, flavored salts such as garlic and onion. One large pickle alone has 1,000 milligrams of sodium.

Need more? One 3-ounce serving of baked chicken has 86 milligrams of sodium. A single 3-ounce piece of (fast-food-type) fried chicken has 500 milligrams. One small frozen chicken pot pie has 863 milligrams! I think you're getting the point. As processing increases, so does the sodium content.

Do You Salt Your Potatoes?

So why are all these numbers I'm giving you so important? It's simple. Too much salt in your diet may lead to high blood pressure, and can increase your risk of stroke, heart attack, and kidney failure. Just to be sure you're not overdoing it, avoid items containing more than 150 milligrams per serving. Try these helpful hints:

- ♥ Use less salt in cooking.
- ♥ Check labels for sodium information.
- ♥ Do not add salt at the table.
- ♥ Try using other blends of spices, herbs, lemon or lime juice or fresh garlic.
- ♥ Eat fresh rather than processed foods as often as possible.
- ♥ If you must salt, consider using Kosher or sea salt, as it is course and less is needed.

Sugar... How Sweet It Is — NOT!

Natural sugars, such as those found in fresh fruits, are the best forms of complex carbohydrates, because they are loaded with minerals and vitamins. Simple sugars are those found in soft drinks, baked goods, candies, and sweets. A single twelve ounce can of regular soda offers about nine to 10 teaspoons of sugar! In fact, the American diet is rich with these refined sugars that fill foods and beverages with flavor, but add very few vitamins and minerals.

Cutting back on foods high in refined sugar is a major step toward wellness. Always check food labels for the ingredients, as the first three ingredients listed constitute most of that food item. And learn to be a sugar sleuth. There are a number of technical names that indicate sugar, so watch out for them. Some of the more common listings include dextrose, lactose, sucrose, honey, and corn syrup.

If you simply must have processed foods with sugar, know your numbers. When choosing breakfast cereals, for example, look for those that contain no more than seven grams of sugar per serving, and try limiting your sweets to one to three *servings* per week. This is particularly important if you're watching your weight, as one teaspoon of sugar has fifteen calories. That can add up pretty quickly to unwanted pounds

Vitamins And Minerals

Whole volumes have been written about vitamins and minerals, and even more ink has been spilled in the debate over whether or not supplements are necessary. Some experts say that if you eat a proper diet, supplements are inordinate and can possibly even be harmful. Others insist that few people in our culture do eat an adequate diet, and that most of us should at least be taking a multivitamin supplement. It's beyond the scope of this author to make that decision for you. What's not in question, however, is that vitamins and minerals are essential nutrients. Like water, they contain no calories, but we need them to maintain good health.

For example, our bones and teeth are composed of minerals — chiefly calcium, but also phosphorous, magnesium, and fluoride. Minerals are also involved in many of our life-sustaining chemical processes, such as metabolism and the transmission of nerve impulses. Vitamins, of course, also contribute to our bodies' biochemical processes. Thanks to significant improvements in our diet over the past century — a direct result of utilizing what science has learned about vitamins' role in our health — it has become more rare for people in our society to suffer the deficiencies that were once common causes of disability or death.

The best way to acquire vitamins and minerals is through food. Recent research, however, is uncovering evidence that some vitamins have additional health-promoting potential if consumed in larger amounts than those we normally get from our food. This is not a signal to rush out to the local health-food store and buy out its supply of the latest trendy mega-supplement. Always check with your health-care practitioner, and/ or consult with a qualified nutritional expert, before embarking on any supplemental vitamin / mineral regimen. Remember, it is most ideal to get your vitamins and minerals through food sources. In my recipes, I have added some helpful tips for understanding foods that offer greater amounts of vitamins and minerals. Also see Appendix A, at the back of the book, for detailed information on the recommended daily amounts of important vitamins and minerals.

Getting to the heart of what matters really can make a difference, and with that, we'll conclude this chapter. But what's that, you say? We forgot to discuss fat? Well, that, my fine friends, warrants a chapter all to itself!

CHAPTER ELEVEN:
GET TO "KNOW" FAT...
ANYTHING THAT "MOOOOVES" HAS IT!

Nowadays, we seem to view fat as something that's destructive, unhealthy, and altogether unattractive. Think about it: can you remember hearing the word "fat" used as a positive description of anything? Probably not. There has been a movement by some toward removing fat from our diet entirely, and that's really a shame. The truth is, in *small* amounts and *proper types*, fat is a necessary nutrient and a concentrated source of energy. In meager quantity, fat can be our friend, and should be treated as such, rather than making it the scapegoat for our own lack of controlled moderation.

Our bodies use fat to store energy until we need it. This fat "reserve" can help keep our bodies running if we are in short supply of food. Like the battery in a car, fat is there to provide a "boost" when we haven't eaten anything in awhile. It also surrounds our vital organs, helping to protect them from trauma and keeping them warm when the weather gets too cold (or when Aunt Martha turns the air conditioning down to "meat-locker" setting to compensate for her hot flashes).

Fat is also necessary for healthy skin and hair. (Read the contents label on your favorite conditioner, and you'll think you've stumbled upon a cross between a refinery

It's important that you learn to examine the profile of each product you eat, analyzing fat and calories. It helps to think of your body as a "tightwad" that would rather store fat than spend (burn) it.

and an Appalachian cookbook.) Fat protects our nervous system, builds tissues, forms hormones, and carries vitamins to our cells. So, then, why has fat developed the reputation of a vicious dietary villain?

In a poignant sense, some may joke about themselves or others who are obviously never in short supply of their fat "reserve". But it's really nothing to joke about. Through diets exceedingly high in fats, many of us eat as if we may end up on a deserted island starving for food. In fact, Americans have the highest incidence of heart disease and obesity, mainly because our bodies are building up unnecessary levels of fat.

What's the solution? We simply need to educate ourselves, practice moderation, and stop eating the amount of fat equivalent to almost a whole stick of butter every day. We actually need to ingest much less (and only unsaturated) fat to perform all the important functions just discussed. So let's quit being such reactionaries, and get to know fat. Just approach it as you would any other friend that you like to visit on a *limited* basis. (Maybe like Aunt Martha...?)

First, let's discuss just what fat *is*. Whereas calories are units of measure for heat or actual energy, fats are elements that provide concentrated sources of energy, calculated by weight in grams. Generally, each gram of fat supplies about nine calories, or approximately 3,500 calories to one pound. While a calorie represents an immediately available source of energy, a gram of fat must first be broken down before the energy is in a form that the body can utilize. Unfortunately, this part of the process isn't always very efficient, and the body typically retains a significant portion of the fat, rather than converting it all to energy. Therefore, it follows that within a healthy diet, your calories from fat must be kept to a bare minimum.

So why have some of us become so obsessed with completely cutting the fat out of our lives? It is obviously an over-reaction to our long-established habit of ingesting far more than we actually need. In some areas, such as the Deep South, there are some who feel that "If it ain't fried, it ain't food." While this is, of course, stated in jest, it reflects a mindset that is not terribly uncommon throughout the country. It's interesting that in many other countries around the world, there is an amazingly lower incidence of heart disease, primarily attributable to dietary customs. We've been subconsciously taught by traditional eating habits — and by modern fast-food marketing efforts — that the tastiest foods just so happen to be those that are also high in fat. It is this mindset that needs to be reversed by adopting moderation and good dietary sense. I call it eating with your heart and mind.

To give you an illustration of what we have been doing to ourselves, consider this: The average American spends over 6,000 hours of his or her life...EATING! As I mentioned in an earlier chapter, in the course of a day, we usually choose between 12 and 15 food selections. Most of us typically consume between 80 and 100 grams of fat every day. That is equivalent to an entire stick of butter. (Bet you thought I was exaggerating about the butter thing, didn't you? I wasn't!) Most of us wouldn't even consider sitting down and gobbling a whole stick of butter, yet on an average day we virtually do just that.

While fats are digested slowly, sustaining a relatively constant blood sugar level over a period of five to six hours, the excess amounts that we eat are stored. Unfortunately, however, most of this excess fat tends to accumulate in all the wrong places, rather than providing our bodies with any benefits. The habit of eating such high amounts of dietary fat has been linked to such unwanted effects as high blood-cholesterol levels, heart disease, and some types of cancer. While large thighs and a potbelly may be more visually apparent, these other effects, the "silent killers", should be cause for even more concern. So, do yourself (if not your doctors' retirement plans) a favor, and *read between the grams*"!

The Acid Test

Dietary fat is made up of fatty acids. These fatty acids are divided into four major categories, according to the chemical structure of the fat molecules:

- ♥ *Saturated fatty acids* emanate mainly from foods of animal origins (including dairy products) and many oils.
- ♥ *Trans fatty acids* are formed as a result of hydrogenation, a man-made process.
- ♥ *Monounsaturated fatty acids* are found in both animals and plants, but originate primarily from plants.
- ♥ *Polyunsaturated fatty acids* are found in plant oils.

Strive to limit your intake of saturated fats to a maximum of one to two grams per serving in each food item that you consume. Your daily maximum should not exceed 30 to 40 grams of total fat (that's a little over one ounce, for our metrically-challenged readers), and, at the absolute maximum, 10 to 12 grams of saturated fat. These amounts, however, are appropriate only for "normal" circumstances, assuming that you are in excellent health. It is highly recommended that you successfully maintain your fat intake *below* the levels recommended by the American Heart Association if you have any related health concerns.

Here's a good guideline for limiting your fat intake. Try to choose foods with three grams of fat (or less) for every 100 calories. I know what you're thinking: that your choices range from sawdust to lint — or things that taste like one of these culinary "treats". Trust me: there are now, more than ever, lots of wonderful things to eat that won't clog your pipes! We'll go into that in more detail later.

The Dangerous Masked Bandit

Probably the most unhealthy type of fat is *trans fat*. Until the end of the 20th century, not much emphasis was openly placed on this markedly harmful ingredient. This man-made artery-clogger is the result of the *hydrogenation* process. Adding hydrogen to vegetable oil or its derivatives alters the molecular structure of unsaturated fat, changing it to a saturated type of fat that is even more damaging than regular saturated fat.

As is the case with many preservatives, one reason for hydrogenation is to increase the product's shelf life and maintain flavor. Another widely used purpose is to thicken vegetable oil into margarine and related products. The real "wolf in sheep's clothing" appears when certain soft tub margarines, for example, are marketed as having little or no cholesterol. Manufacturers can legitimately state this if it is made with certain vegetable oils, but *don't be fooled into thinking it's safe*. Products may be free of cholesterol, but the trans fat resulting from "partially hydrogenated" (or "hydrogenized") ingredients is typically more hazardous.

Why are trans fats even worse than saturated fats? Unlike saturated fat, which can slowly be broken down over time, the body cannot easily break down and eliminate the fat created by these manually manipulated chemical changes. Therefore, this resulting trans fat will tend to linger and lodge in the body much longer, threatening the cardiovascular system and promoting weight gain.

Many butters, frozen or dried foods, cookies, doughnuts, crackers, and other "processed" foods are also hydrogenated. In fact, this process is applied to a surprising variety of edibles. While it may not be practical to completely avoid products that include the words "hydrogenated" or "hydrogenized," certainly try to use them sparingly. Watch your labels, and only choose products that divulge these words as close to the bottom of the ingredient list as possible. And here's another great tip: If the combination of all saturated and unsaturated fats don't add up to the *total* fat listed on a label, guess where the rest is probably coming from! As a side-note, many restaurants re-use their cooking oil, and in the process, increase the levels of trans fat. A typical extra-large order of French fries can contain approximately 19 grams of this potential killer.

Sometimes, We All Need A Hero...

T here exists yet another type of fat, a fatty acid called *omega-3*, which has been a source of some excitement among nutritionists and health-conscious cooks. This type of polyunsaturated fat has been shown to have characteristics that make blood platelets less likely to clot in the blood vessels. It has been reported that these fatty acids may actually help reduce the risk of artery blockage. High levels of omega-3's are found in many types of seafood, such as salmon, tuna, herring, and rainbow trout.

Of all the fats, Omega Man is our best friend, and could be a typical hero in a comic book that a zany dietician might buy for his or her kids (who will no doubt grow up disliking their over-zealous parent, and will probably end up attending wild lard-eating parties in college as a form of rebellion). (*Editor's Note*: This is one case where the parent may just outlive the kids!)

Sole Food

S hellfish is one of those unusual foods that is high in cholesterol, but filled with unsaturated fat and omega-3 fatty acids. Seafood is generally low in calories. Fish is an excellent source of protein and a tasty alternative to red meat. The seafoods that are the lowest in fat and highest in vitamin B, iron, and zinc include: flounder, cod, sole, shrimp, crab, and scallops. Cold water fish are known to be fattier fish. When using canned seafood (tuna being a common example), be sure that you purchase products that are packed only in water, and not oil.

A steady diet of four to six ounces of seafood, twice weekly, has been proven to diminish the rate of plaque build-up in the heart vessels, or even dissolve plaque. However, always be aware of the storage date. If the seafood has any kind of odor, never, never use it. Also, use caution and good judgment whenever eating raw seafood.

Use The Skill, Not Just Your Will

As I've said before, keeping your intake of dietary fat at a healthy level should not be viewed as a major battle. The effort should involve more education than willpower. Besides, with the mind control techniques that work best for you, fatty foods will probably no longer be that much of a desire. Being aware of what your body actually needs, and selecting dishes that meet — but don't dramatically exceed — those needs, while satisfying your cravings, is not the daunting task it may seem. The more you know about your body and the foods you put into it, the easier it will be to make healthy choices that are satisfying to your palate as well as your health. In other words, knowledge feeds power, and subsequently leads to a lifestyle change that can last a (longer) lifetime!

Remember again that calories still count. The maximum amount of fat considered healthy in your diet is based on the number of calories you consume daily, as well as your normal activity level. The American Heart Association recommends that no more than 30 percent of your total daily calories come from fat.

I can hear a few of the die-hards out there saying: "All right! If I take in 10,000 calories a day, it's okay to eat a whole pound of butter!" Wrong again, oh Clogged One! Your daily caloric *intake* needs to hover right around the amount of calories you *burn* in a day. If your most strenuous activity involves punching buttons on the keyboard or remote, you can safely eat all the sawdust and lint you want. (Just kidding about sawdust and lint being safe!) On the other hand, you'd certainly best lay off the bon-bons, eclairs, and peanut-butter-filled chocolates, to name just a few. Your personal condition, lifestyle (including diet and exercise regimens), family history, and goals are important factors that must be considered when determining the variables for your proper caloric and fat intake.

As you are probably aware, there are other important reasons to watch your diet besides to decrease your risk of heart disease or cancer. Obesity, for example, is a major problem in our country. Even though we are eating lighter and leaner than ever, the United States is still ranked highest in the world for obesity (besides being relatively high on the list in the percentage of the world population who suffer from heart disease). While we'd like to think that we are the "tops", these rankings aren't anything to boast about. The fact that we "excel" in these areas won't win us any great acclaim, unless you count the nice things people say about you in your obituary column. Too bad, you usually aren't around to read that, anyway. The unhappy truth is, obesity is one of the leading risk factors for many diseases.

So what causes overweight? The simple answer is that extra weight is the result of taking in more calories than you burn off. Your body will count calories, even if you don't. That's why it is important to establish your fat-gram budget, and resolve to stick to it. It's all part of your resolution to make the rest of your life a quest for health and happiness.

Again, don't view this as a temporary change, or it will always feel like a task that you are being forced to perform against your will. That's why most people who "go on a diet" end up gaining back as much weight as they lose, or more. They suffer through the "diet", only to "reward" themselves later, by eating all the things they were dreaming about while they suffered. Instead of riding this dietary and emotional see-saw, make a permanent commitment to seeking out things that both your palate and your body can enjoy, and the battle will become a joyous dance.

Learn To Be A Food Sleuth

It's important that you learn to examine the profile of each product you eat, analyzing fat and calories. It helps to think of your body as a "tightwad" that would rather store fat than spend (burn) it. Realize, too, that it takes twice as much energy to burn off one gram of fat as it does to burn one gram of carbohydrate or protein. While calories are actually units of potential energy, those calories that you don't convert to energy through exercise will end up being stored in all those wrong places we talked about earlier, contributing to the visible — and less visible — effects we all would rather avoid.

As you can probably deduce by now, to consume only the fat that your body requires, you want to choose strictly polyunsaturated and monounsaturated oils (of plant origin, *excluding* coconut, palm, kernel, cottonseed, and oils of those types). A good start would be to add non-stick vegetable cooking spray and fat-free butter substitutes, including those in pump sprays, to your pantry stock.

The game is a-food, Watson!

TIME FOR AN OIL CHANGE!

SATURATED FATS / TRANS FATS

Fats Originating from Animals or Man-Made Processes

CAN CONTRIBUTE TO ELEVATED BLOOD CHOLESTEROL AND TRIGLYCERIDES, AS WELL AS CARDIOVASCULAR DISEASE AND WEIGHT GAIN

Some sources are:

♥ VISIBLE OR "HIDDEN" FAT IN MEAT (BEEF, LAMB, PORK, SAUSAGE, BACON, HOT DOGS)
♥ DAIRY PRODUCTS MADE FROM WHOLE MILK OR CREAM (BUTTER, WHOLE MILK, CHEESE, CREAM, SOUR CREAM, ICE CREAM)
♥ COCONUT AND PALM (KERNEL) OILS
♥ COCOA BUTTER (IN CHOCOLATE)
♥ "HYDROGENATED" OR HARDENED VEGETABLE OILS (IN PEANUT BUTTER, STICK MARGARINE, CRACKERS, COMMERCIAL BAKERY PRODUCTS)

UNSATURATED FATS

POLYUNSATURATED:

Fats Usually of Plant Origin

IN MODERATE AMOUNTS, CAN HELP TO LOWER CERTAIN BLOOD CHOLESTEROL

Some sources are:

♥ SAFFLOWER, CORN, SUNFLOWER, SOYBEAN, COTTONSEED OILS
♥ SOFT TUB MARGARINE WITH LIQUID OIL

MONOUNSATURATED:

Fats of Plant Origin

IN MODERATE AMOUNTS, CAN HELP TO LOWER CERTAIN BLOOD CHOLESTEROL

Some sources are:

♥ OLIVE OIL, OLIVES
♥ PEANUTS, PEANUT OIL
♥ CANOLA OIL

Some of the fat-free spreads taste great on bread, and the nonfat "squeezables" are excellent for foods such as baked potatoes. We have taken a particular liking to the pump spray products, because they offer the taste and satisfaction of butter or margarine, even though they are diluted. Furthermore, they have become assets to many low-fat or non-fat recipes, especially for maintaining moisture and aiding in the melting of certain nonfat cheeses. Butter powders can also provide the butter flavor for baked potatoes or popcorn. Try to select vegetable sprays that are made from canola oil, as this has the lowest percentage of saturated fat. Safflower, olive, corn, or sunflower oils are the next best choices. Again, avoid tropical oils, such as palm, kernel, or coconut oils, as they have high amounts of saturated fat. And don't automatically assume that by using the sprays, you're home-free when it comes to being fat-free. Don't overdo it, because some of the cooking spray labels indicate that their serving size is based upon an actual spraying time of only *one-third of one second.*

Okay, so how do you become a savvy food sleuth? How do you really "know fat" when you see it? In some foods, fats are noticeable and easily apparent. Remember that pot of chili they served at the company picnic, the one with the pools of orange stuff floating on top? Easy to spot the culprit there. Many foods, however, have a high fat content that you can't detect at a glance. Two tablespoons of peanut butter, for example, have about sixteen grams (about half of what you should eat in a whole day) of fat. Many baked goods and candies (alas, especially chocolate) contain oils, and can have a high fat content. Check and compare foods. When you find a brand or product that has a low fat-gram count and a flavor that your family enjoys, stock up on it. And if you happen to find a brand of chocolate bar that tastes great, yet is fat-free, please write to me… Some things are still especially elusive.

Standards With Heart

The American Heart Association was founded in 1924, and is the oldest and largest non-profit voluntary health organization dedicated to reducing disability and death due to cardiovascular disease and stroke. The following dietary guidelines are recommended by the American Heart Association to reduce blood pressure and cholesterol levels, and aid in the lowering of risk factors for heart disease and stroke.

- ♥ Total fat intake should be less than 30% of total daily calories.
- ♥ Saturated fat should be less than 10% of total daily calories.
- ♥ Polyunsaturated fat intake should be less than 10% of total daily calories.
- ♥ Cholesterol should not exceed 300 milligrams per day.
- ♥ Carbohydrate intake should make up 50% or more of our daily calories. Most carbohydrates should come from "complex" carbohydrates.
- ♥ Protein should provide the rest of our daily calories.
- ♥ Sodium should be less than 3 grams, or 3000 milligrams, daily.
- ♥ Total calories consumed should be the amount necessary to maintain your recommended body weight.
- ♥ A wide variety of foods should be consumed to gain a balance of nutrients.

All of the above information is based on total calories per day, not per meal. Please remember, however, that all of these amounts are intended for average, healthy people. They are benchmarks for balanced nourishment under average circumstances, which also include a routine of regular aerobic exercise.

If you don't fall into that "average, healthy" category, the suggested amounts need to be adjusted accordingly. For example, if you have hypertension (high blood pressure), chances are that your doctor will strongly recommend a much lower sodium (salt) intake than listed. If you have had a personal or family history of heart disease or diabetes, or are concerned with controlling weight gain, it may be well advised to strive for lower fat intake levels than those recommended above. At least, you may want to set them as absolute maximums, reserved for those rare, totally uncontrollable situations like the holiday parties at the office. On the other hand, if you have a problem maintaining a high enough body weight — but are otherwise perfectly healthy — you may be advised to increase your intake of calories from certain sources of food. The rest of us will, of course, have no pity on you for it, so be discreet, and don't rub it in our faces!

As you can see, while there are excellent standards and guidelines to follow, there are no hard and fast rules about calorie and fat intake. All the guidelines in the world won't do you any good if you don't adjust the recommended amounts to your own personal condition and activity level. Common sense, along with the information provided here, should help you plot a course for the healthiest body you can have. Furthermore, if you embrace a proper and healthy outlook, your improved eating habits won't feel restrictive.

CHAPTER TWELVE:
LICK THE PROBLEM, NOT YOUR PLATE

I f you recall from earlier chapters, in his "old life", Les was addicted to eating. He ate whatever he had a taste for, and as much as he desired. As difficult as it was for him to change, he conquered the problem on his own, by personalizing some basic psychological techniques. These methods stem from the powerful human belief system, and as you read ahead, we invite you to think about how you can apply them in your own life.

As we start to empower ourselves, we begin to realize that we are in control of our eating habits.

One generic and very old secret of success is based upon the premise that conscious thought fuels one of the most powerful forces known in the universe: the human sub-conscious mind. Our subconscious does not know the difference between the truth and a lie. It simply believes and acts upon whatever it is *told* by the *conscious* mind. Just as a computer, it will produce significant action and results, but only on the basis of its informational input.

A common example of this can be seen in people who are raised in an especially positive environment. Most of these children ultimately grow up to be confident, happy, and successful adults. Since infancy, they con-stantly received genuine love and enthusiastic praise for even their small achievements, and were always clear about the strong bond in their relationship with their parents. They developed self-confidence through a happy and supportive upbringing, and high moral standards from good role models. One can easily see the connection between positive self-esteem and unlimited accomplishments. In contrast, as we examine the growing number of criminals, it is often noted that these emotional needs were not fulfilled during their early years. Among many of these individuals, there is, unfortunately, a common pattern of negative childhood experiences, sometimes resultant from poor or absent role models, neglect, or even abuse.

We believe both of these extremes illustrate the power of the subconscious mind. The happy and confident people believed what was communicated to them: that they were smart, creative, kind, and all-around great people. Their powerful subconscious drivers performed accordingly, and activated their "cruise control" to success. Similarly, many misguided souls who believe negatively about themselves eventually seem to find a way to fulfill their "convictions".

The great news is that any of us can rise up from negative experiences and embrace new and better ways. We must first convince ourselves that we are worthy of success. Because our subconscious has no power to reason, but simply believes and acts upon what it hears, we are all born with enormous power that many of us never discover during our lifetime.

Digesting Conscious Mind Control...
A Weighty Concept

We are essentially all born equal, and have similar potential. As we start to empower ourselves, we begin to realize that we are in control of our eating habits. Thereby, we can allow ourselves to overcome food's control over us. Read on to discover how Les did just that.

Feeling Is Believing!

Les was able to employ the basic but powerful features of the subconscious through the technique of *conscious mind control*. To easily "digest" this technique for making a lifestyle change, here is Les' "hands-on" (or, rather, "tongues-on") exercise. Try it for yourself.

♥ Plan to have a juicy steak or large order of French fries. Before eating these foods, thoroughly brush your teeth (your dentist will be grateful). Just prior to taking your first bite, run your tongue over your teeth, to experience the clean sensation. When you have finished eating, feel your teeth again with your tongue, and notice the coating of a pasty, gritty film. This is where saturated fat lives up to its highly accurate name. Not even a beverage will easily wash that sticky film away.

♥ Les realized, as we hope you do, that much of this harmful "film" that is left on your teeth is similar to the same substance that builds up on the inside walls of our blood vessels. That thought alone made him squeamish, since these vessels support our very existence. Les would no more have the desire to eat foods with these harmful contents than any thinking person would skydive without a parachute. Self-destruction is self-destruction, no matter which method you choose.

♥ Using this conscious mental imagery, Les allowed his subconscious to do the work, directing his taste buds to *actually crave* better food choices. By always keeping these images in the forefront, he almost completely eliminated the temptation for harmful, high-fat foods. Instead, *positive feelings* of enjoyment and contentment flowed from consuming his tasty, new-found, clean, and healthy choices! Thus the battle was won. No longer were deprivation and willpower necessary tools for Les' success. Convincing himself to believe what he knew was right, along with using powerful imagery techniques, created an automatic reaction of *distaste* at the mere *thought* of "unclean" foods.

Worth Your Weight In Gold

To develop a genuine love for healthy foods, the first challenge we need to overcome is the mental block that was self-imposed by many of us, years ago. Much of our *past* is the reason for our present habits. Our old mindset is actually the root of our inability to enjoy certain replacement foods "at first taste" — healthy foods that we know are better for us. Our likes and dislikes are better understood by viewing these taste conceptions as mere habits. So cheer up! With a little desire, habits *can* be re-examined and *can* be changed, as soon as we decide to do so.

With the proven benefit of mind control, you too can re-program yourself to be naturally turned off by unhealthy foods, both emotionally and physically. It's all in your mind, even though it may feel more like it's in your mouth and stomach! When eating something "unclean" (such as a high-fat Alfredo sauce), visualize the harmful substance, some of which is likely clinging to the inside of your vessels, long after your taste buds have finished having their party. View it in your mind as the threat to your life that it really is. Consider that (regardless of the taste), it may be destroying the only body you will ever have. Looking at oily, buttery, fried, and otherwise fatty foods in this manner can help you develop a genuine dislike for these harmful selections. This new viewpoint can result in the desire to intentionally *want* to avoid them.

So how do you know when you have achieved this mindset successfully? The answer is, when you actually *enjoy* the taste of "clean foods" and are truthfully turned off by the idea of allowing "unclean food" to enter your mouth. When you *know* that you are controlling your food choices, they will not be in control of you. At that point, congratulate yourself for no longer being a "slave to the crave"!

A powerful tool for motivation is taking a look toward your future. By envisioning the future with health and happiness, you are giving each day more meaning and value. Your gratitude and desire for "life" gives you the will to do whatever it takes to hold on to it. In other words, merely *wishing* to be around to see your children grow up will not necessarily make it happen. On the other hand, practicing good health can easily place this dream more within your reach. As you know from the anecdote I shared in an earlier chapter, Les' love for his family was his best motivation to stay alive and healthy. He uses these positive mental image techniques to picture his children growing up. He imagines himself playing with his future grandchildren.

He even uses this method for going that "extra mile" when running out of steam during exercise. The extra energy he needs is somehow magically available when he creates a vivid visualization of his circulatory system working to produce a perfect balance. His mental illustration is very graphic, as he clearly imagines his HDL (good cholesterol) sweeping away any undesirable residue from the vessels within his body.

We all realize what we have to live for, and by making daily healthful choices, we are truly living. Looking forward to tomorrow makes getting there so much more exciting and worthwhile. Knowing the alternative, I ask you… is a pizza worth all that much? *Really?* I don't think so!

I hope you now understand that your conscious thoughts propel your subconscious mind, which in turn governs most of your decisions and actions. You decide that *you* are in charge and that *you* have the power to choose what your taste buds will call "mmm, mmm… good!" Les analogizes this power to one of the themes from the movie, *Star Wars*: **We all have the power of "The Force"!**

And remember, as with any addiction that didn't develop overnight, habits do take time to change. Research has shown that to break any long-standing habit can take as long as four to six weeks (or occasionally longer). As many of my clients have found, the longer you *delight* in "clean" foods, and adjust your taste buds away from the highly saturated greasy types, the less you will miss them. Better still, the less you will probably even be able to tolerate them. So stay focused, but give yourself time to adapt to your lifestyle changes. You'll be surprised how many other aspects of your life will improve as well!

> **Little cookie in my hand**
> **Will I ever understand**
> **That eating you from pure frustration**
> **Will not help my situation**
> **When I'm in a saddened mood**
> **Nothing changes with this food**
> **What I really have to do... is ask myself what's eating you?**
>
> *Author unknown*

I can encourage you, guide you, and inspire you with Les' and my experiences, but the truly amazing part of all this will come *when you see these principles actually work for you*. Just remember that you have a great deal more to gain than a better state of mind and body. You just might be saving your own life! So…*"May the POWER be with you!"*

CHAPTER THIRTEEN:
EATING FOR THE HEALTH OF IT
(EVEN IF YOU DON'T HAVE DESIGNER GENES!)

I am often asked what people can do if their personal genetics and/or family history put them at increased risk for various diseases. These days, for example, many people come from a high-risk gene pool for heart disease and many high-incidence cancers. Does this mean they should just sit back and wait for the inevitable?

Of course not! The good news is that there is a lot you can do to help yourself, even if you are in one of these high-risk groups. Having a family history of disease should not discourage you from practicing healthy eating habits. On the contrary, it should act as an even stronger message of the necessity to practice prevention.

As I've mentioned before, it's interesting that there are many parallels between the suggested diets for helping to prevent both cancer and heart disease. As you certainly know by now, research has shown that diet can have a significant effect on our health. While there may always be unknown factors that influence our destiny, there are also certain control measures that have been found to lower our risk factors for various diseases. For instance, high fiber, low fat, and plenty of fruits and vegetables on a regular basis can have a considerable ben-

...research has shown that diet can have a significant effect on our health. While there may always be unknown factors... there are also certain control measures that have been found to lower our risk factors for various diseases.

eficial effect. From what I've learned through my personal experience with cancer, these tips represent a brief overview that can start you on the road to effective dietary changes for reducing your cancer risks.

Six Steps Toward Prevention

1. *"Five a Day" with fruits and vegetables.* These are the top ten fruits and veggies that are rich in cancer-fighting vitamins and fiber:

- ♥ Broccoli
- ♥ Cantaloupe
- ♥ Carrots
- ♥ Kale
- ♥ Mango
- ♥ Pumpkin
- ♥ Red Bell Pepper
- ♥ Spinach
- ♥ Strawberries
- ♥ Sweet Potato

2. *Fill up on fiber.* Regularly eat foods like beans, whole grains, peas, cabbage and cauliflower, pasta or brown rice and high-fiber cereal.

3. *Forget the fat.* Choose low-fat or fat-free foods as a regular habit (heard that one before?).

4. *Shake off salt and nitrates.* Eliminate high-sodium foods such as hot dogs, bacon, and foods that are salt-cured or smoked.

5. *Abstain from alcohol whenever possible.* While there have been reports claiming that a very small amount of alcohol can be beneficial for lowering the risk of heart disease, it is also felt that alcohol in any quantity can increase the risk of cancer.

6. *Add anti-oxidants.* Include full servings of foods rich in vitamins A, C, and E. Vitamin A is found in foods with deep yellow and dark green color. Vitamin C is found in citrus fruits, tomatoes and green peppers, and vi-

tamin E is found in green leafy vegetables and whole-grain products. A whole-grain product is one that still has its outer covering, containing the grain's fiber, vitamins and minerals. Certainly, supplements are available for just about everything, but there has always been a contention from medical authorities that the best sources of vitamins and minerals are foods that sport them naturally.

A Bounty Of Benefits

I am often asked for a breakdown of foods that carry specific benefits. Here is an interesting list of categories, and just a few of the foods that can offer characteristics to fulfill them:

Energy Foods

Fresh Fruit or Fruit Juice
Whole Wheat Bread Sticks
Raisins
Yogurt
Soft Baked Pretzel
Baked Potato
Pita Bread
Graham Crackers
Juice Bars
English Muffins
Carrots
Angel Food Cake

Cancer Resistance

(The emphasis is on cruciferous vegetables, which are from the cabbage family)

Broccoli
Brussels Sprouts
Cabbage
Cauliflower
Kale
Mustard Greens
Rutabaga
Turnips

Relaxing Foods

Vanilla Wafers
Animal Crackers
Sherbet or Low Fat Yogurt
Warm Soups
Fresh Fruit (cut up)
Bagel and Jam
Tea
Fat Free Pudding

Fiber Foods

Apples
Bananas
Blackberries
Blueberries
Brussels Sprouts
Carrots
Cherries
Cooked Beans and Peas
Dates
Figs
Kiwi Fruit
Oranges
Pears
Prunes
Raspberries
Spinach
Strawberries
Sweet Potatoes

Iron-Rich Foods

Tuna
Tofu
Turkey (no skin)
Baked Potato
Raisins
Cooked Broccoli
Garbanzo Beans
Steamed Clams

High in Vitamin D

Salmon
Sardines
Herring
Fortified Milk

High in Vitamin A

Apricots
Cantaloupe
Carrots
Kale
Leaf Lettuce
Mango
Pumpkin
Romaine Lettuce
Spinach
Sweet Potatoes
Winter Squash

High in Vitamin C

Apricots
Broccoli
Brussels Sprouts
Cabbage
Cantaloupe
Cauliflower
Chili Peppers
Collards
Grapefruit
Honey Dew Melon
Kiwi Fruit
Mango
Orange
Pineapple
Plum
Potato with Skin
Spinach
Strawberries
Bell Peppers
Tangerine
Tomatoes
Watermelon

Don't make the mistake of letting your genetic "baggage" keep you from your journey to good health. You can't command everything, but you can take an amazing amount of control of your health — and your life — by choosing your foods wisely.

CHAPTER FOURTEEN:
TIPS, TRICKS, CLUES AND WHAT TO DO'S

S o far, I've been stressing the need for a sensible approach to your eating habits. I've spoken about how to align your priorities and fine-tune your mind. Now, it's time to get down to the nitty-gritty of actually making the changes. I promised that it wouldn't feel like punishment, and with the right mindset, it won't. In this chapter, you will find lots of "little" things you can do to make your healthy foods more satisfying.

...keeping preparation times short, and ingredients relatively simple, were among my goals while developing this book. At the same time, I also wanted to make the dishes delicious and visually appealing.

Since I admittedly am not an avowed "June Cleaver", that is, a "spend-my-life-in-the-kitchen" type of woman, it followed that keeping preparation times short, and ingredients relatively simple, were among my goals while developing this book. At the same time, I also wanted to make the dishes delicious and visually appealing, so I applied the principle of KISS ("Keep It Smart & Simple") to each and every recipe. I was delighted with how well they measured up to (and often surpassed) my husband's picky taste standards. I hope they will do the same for you.

Here are more tips, tricks, rules, and tools (not necessarily in order of importance):

1. Before beginning any recipe, read over the recipe carefully, and collect all the ingredients.

2. Make sure your counter tops and cutting boards are clean and bacteria-free.

3. Purchase only cookware and appliances that meet your cooking and lifestyle needs (I'll give you some suggestions later on in this list). While the "inside-the-shell egg scrambler" might have been an intriguing idea on the infomercial at 3 AM, you might discover that it takes up room on your shelf, and is probably removed only during semi-annual dusting expeditions.

Pull out your old bridal shower gifts, and look up the "Trifle" dessert recipe, so that you can put that bowl to work!

Invest in a food processor of your choice to make chopping and blending easy. Purchase a size that is practical in meeting *your* needs. For our family, I prefer the "Little Oscar" by Sunbeam. Keep your food processor out or available in the kitchen, so that you will already have it set up whenever you need to use it.

I had the brilliant idea to use my food processor to make salmon croquettes one time, but got a bit carried away. The croquettes came out absolutely beautiful, but were the consistency of hockey pucks. Moral: Learn how to use — but not over-use — your food processor.

---

4. Check the expiration and shelf-life dates of your ingredients. Note that some low-fat and fat-free foods are not as high in preservatives as traditional processed food items, and therefore may not last as long in your pantry.

5. Make sure that your proper cookware is handy (not in the dishwasher, waiting for Mr. "It's-not-my-turn-to-wash" to turn it on), and keep a good set of measuring spoons and cups available for both liquid and dry measuring. In fact, it's a good idea to keep all of your most commonly-used accessories readily at hand, particularly those that you use regularly for your low-fat regimen. Doing this will also help to promote your habit of healthy cooking and eating.

6. Use equipment that offers time-saving efficiency and lends itself to low-fat cooking (allowing most of the fat to drip out of the food, while cooking in flavor without heavy butters and sauces). Here are some basics:

- ♥ Roasting Rack
- ♥ Steamer
- ♥ Two-part Meat Loaf Pan
- ♥ Fat Skimmer and Strainer
- ♥ Blender or Food Processor
- ♥ Pressure Cooker
- ♥ Gravy Skimmer
- ♥ Salad Spinner
- ♥ Plastic Storage Bags
- ♥ Nonstick Cookware and Bakeware

7. Learn, and practice, healthy cooking methods, such as:

♥ *Roasting:* A dry-heat method, usually done uncovered in an oven. Try to place your meat or poultry on a rack within your roasting pan, which will allow the fat to drip off. Cook with a low oven temperature to allow time for the fat to drain off. Do not baste with anything containing fat. Try using fat-free chicken or beef broth. Maintain a small amount of liquid in the bottom of the pan to help prevent burning.

♥ *Steaming:* To cook or heat over boiling water, allowing the steam to circulate without the food contacting the water. This is a healthy way to retain the natural vitamins, minerals and flavors, as long as the proper cooking time is not exceeded.

♥ *Poaching:* To simmer in hot liquids, such as broth, juices, wine or water (seafood is a great low-fat food to poach).

♥ *Broiling:* To cook over (or sometimes under) direct high heat or flame. Broiling with the flame under the food has a greater influence on fat drainage. Less-tender meats will taste better if marinated or tenderized beforehand. Remember, though, to use only fat-free products for marinating. Certain fat-free salad dressings and barbecue or teriyaki sauces work great.

♥ *Baking:* An oven method, usually using a covered cooking dish. Most foods require a little bit of liquid, such as a vegetable cooking spray or nonfat butter spray, during the baking process. To ensure moisture retention, cover the baking pan, and remove it during the last 10 to 12 minutes only.

♥ *Braising or Stewing:* To cook slowly, using either a pan or crock-pot. More liquid is used in stewing than braising. Although this is a slow-cooking method, it can allow the fat to be re-absorbed back into the food. And though this slow method is actually a good way to tenderize tough cuts of meat (for your *"very occasional"* meat-eating!), it's best if you refrigerate overnight, so that some of the fat (that which rises to the top) can be removed. This can be effective when cooking soups with meat or poultry.

♥ *Microwave:* Rapid cooking through electromagnetic energy as a heat source. As long as you're careful to keep all of the food evenly exposed to the microwaves (rotating base-plates are helpful), this is great for thawing or heating foods.

♥ *Barbecue:* Usually outside on a grill with the heat coming from underneath, allowing much of the fat to drip off, if the food is fully cooked (fairly well-done). The principal concept is that an open grill (whether inside or outside) is always the most effective way to allow the fat to drip off, but be careful... especially if you attempt this inside. Fat can catch fire! Also, be aware of reports contending that certain heat sources used for barbecuing can emit carcinogens into the food.

♥ *Sauté:* Cooking food in a small amount of liquid in a pan and stirring occasionally. Fat-free broth, water, or small amounts of vegetable cooking spray are best for keeping the fat content low.

♥ *Stir-fry:* Cooking in a preheated wok or pan on top of the stove with a little vegetable spray, fat-free chicken, or vegetable broth, or a *very limited* amount of oil (don't forget, if you *must* use oil, use only those with the lowest fat content, such as canola or safflower). Meats or vegetables are cooked quickly for about five to eight minutes, stirring continuously. Many woks now come with non-stick finishes, and therefore need very little oil or liquid. (Remember that harder vegetables, such as celery, onions, and carrots, require longer cooking times. Softer vegetables, such as snap peas, mushrooms, bean sprouts, or tomatoes, require shorter cooking.)

♥ *Spanek:* Vertical meat roaster brought to the U.S. from Europe, for cooking meat in the upright position, allowing fat to run off and heat to cook from both the inside and outside, keeping the meat moist, tender, flavorful and evenly cooked.

♥ *Stoneware:* Retains heat and moisture, requires little or no oil or butter, and cooks evenly from top to bottom.

8. Remember that fat-free doesn't mean taste-free. Here are just a few examples of flavorful condiments that are almost (if not completely) fat-free:

♥ Mustard	♥ Taco sauce
♥ Syrup	♥ Cocktail sauce
♥ Ketchup	♥ Picante sauce (Salsa)
♥ Marshmallows	♥ Soy sauce
♥ Honey	♥ Flavor extracts (Vanilla,
♥ Vinegar	etc.)
♥ Marshmallow cream	♥ Balsamic vinegar
♥ Chili sauce (Salsa)	♥ Teriyaki sauce

Remember, however, that some are high in sodium, and some are loaded with sugar, which can easily turn into stored fat if eaten to excess and not burned off with regular exercise!

9. Learn to turn snack attacks to your advantage. Start to develop a taste for healthy snacks. Look for snacks that are low in fat (and have *no* saturated fat), as well as low in cholesterol, sodium, and sugar. This may seem like a difficult task, but manufacturers are making it easier every day.

Here is a partial list of products that can be found in fat-free versions (or with very little fat per serving):

♥ Jell-O™	♥ Crackers
♥ Pretzels	♥ Graham Crackers
♥ Cookies	♥ Tomato Juice
♥ Baked Potato Chips	♥ Rice-Cakes
♥ Corn Chips	♥ Yogurt
♥ Caramel Corn	♥ Apple Sauce
♥ Angel Food Cake	♥ Pita Bread
♥ Flan	♥ Bagel Chips
♥ Dried Fruit	♥ Puddings
♥ Fresh Fruit	♥ Baked Pasta Chips
♥ Microwave Popcorn	♥ Gum-drops
♥ String Cheese	♥ Licorice

Again, however, remember to watch the sugar, sodium, carbohydrates and calories!

10. Spice up your life! Herbs and spices, whether fresh or dried, are a great way to add lots of flavor without adding fat, sodium or sugar. *Herbs* usually refer to the leafy part of plants grown in a temperate climate. *Spices* are primarily seeds, fruits, barks, and roots of tropical origin. While just a limited list, the herbs and spices in the following table are great for enhancing the flavor of any dish.

HERBS	SPICES
Basil: A green leafy aromatic herb with a warm sweet flavor.	**Curry Powder:** A combination of spices originating from India, Indonesia, and Thailand. It can vary in flavor, ranging from mild to hot. Can be added in the beginning or end of a recipe. Curry will blend flavors of many other ingredients.
Bay Leaf: A strong pungent flavor. Add at the end of the cooking process of the dish. Remove before serving.	**Cilantro (fresh coriander):** Fresh clean flavor. As it is cut the flavor pours out. Widely used in Mexican and Thai dishes, but will flavor any salsa, soup, bean dish, marinade, or stew.
Garlic: A natural blood thinner, and can aid in preventing clogged arteries. Crushed or fresh will enhance the flavor of vegetables and many main dishes.	**Turmeric:** Yellowish powdered spice used primarily in Indian and Middle Eastern dishes. Belongs to the ginger family.
Oregano: Strong aromatic odor, does great with Italian dishes and many veggies.	**Ginger:** From the ginger root; native to Asia. Strong flavor, combines great with stir-fry. Powdered dry ginger tastes quite different from fresh ginger root.
Dill: Adds a vegetable flavor.	**Celery Seed:** Adds great flavor to almost any dish.
Rosemary: Shows itself with a scent similar to pine woods. Great on meats, poultry, and potatoes.	**Paprika:** Sweet Hungarian pepper. Paprika should be used on foods that are cooked over a gentle heat to avoid burning.
Marjoram: Comes from the oregano family. Excellent flavor for soups and stews and beans.	**Chili Powder:** Contributes a great deal to foods needing hot flavor. Do not over season or it can be uncomfortably hot and spicy. Used mostly in stews, soups, and Mexican dishes.
Parsley: Blends nicely with the flavors of other herbs. Has a nice clean fresh flavor.	**Mustard:** Dijon type has become one of the more popular mustards and can add zest to sauces, salad dressings, and marinades.
Mint: Cool refreshing flavor. Does great with fruit dishes and teas.	**Fennel Licorice:** Flavored from the plant in the parsley family.
Chive: Green herb with a soft delicate onion flavor.	**Cinnamon:** Familiar sweet popular spice. Can be mixed with sugar or left alone to simmer on a stove for a fresh smell through the house.
Sage: Comes from the leaves of an evergreen shrub. Strong, spicy flavor, used to enhance stuffings and winter vegetables.	**Black Pepper:** Will give zest and warmth to any dish. A fresh pepper grinder adds much, as compared to a regular pepper shaker.

Tip: If substituting dried herbs or spices (instead of fresh), you should increase 3-4 up to triple the amount called for in the recipes. Approximately $^1/_3$ teaspoon ground herbs or spices is equivalent to 1 tablespoon of fresh, and 1 teaspoon of dried herbs or spices also equals 1 tablespoon of fresh. When using fresh, always add them at the end of the cooking period.

11. Explore life's "pastabilities". Here are a few miscellaneous tips for more sure success with pasta (and other) recipes:

♥ Use a large pot, with four quarts of water per pound of pasta (oil is not necessary).

♥ To prevent sticking, bring the water to a boil and then add the pasta; stir frequently with a spoon or pasta fork, being certain to keep the pasta separated.

♥ Dried pasta takes longer to cook than fresh.

♥ Do not overcook. The taste test works well; as soon as you can smoothly bite all the way through, it's done.

♥ Place hot pasta in a warm serving bowl, toss with sauce (or add a small amount of fat-free butter substitute), and serve immediately. Fat-free Italian dressing is a great flavor additive.

♥ Drain pasta immediately and rinse, particularly if it is being used without sauce.

♥ If the pasta is being used in a baked casserole, undercook it very slightly.

♥ Meat and vegetables go well with penne pasta.

♥ Tomato sauce is perfect for vermicelli, capellini or angel hair pasta.

♥ Pasta can be used with vegetables, chicken, meats, seafood, and fat-free cheeses.

12. Know how to prepare fruits and vegetables for cooking.

♥ Wash fresh fruits just before serving or using them to prepare a recipe. They should not be washed earlier, as the moisture will force them to spoil more quickly. To prevent browning or discoloration of apples or citrus fruits, pour lemon juice over the fruit after slicing. One teaspoon should cover two to three apples.

♥ When squeezing fresh lemon juice to prepare a recipe, it is best to squeeze all of the juice from the lemon, and place the juice in a tightly sealed container before storing it in the refrigerator. Use only the amount you need for the recipe, and store the excess.

♥ To make it easier to release oranges, lemons, or limes from their peel, roll them around on the counter with a little downward pressure before cutting into them. Tomatoes can be more easily peeled by popping them in boiling water (otherwise known as blanching) for one minute, and rinsing in cold water.

♥ When cooking with eggplant, leave the skin on (unless the recipe specifically states otherwise), but cut off any irregularities or blemishes.

13. Freezing is a breeze, even if you're cooking for only one or two. For efficiency, and to cover yourself for future tight schedules, prepare more, and cut the extra into appropriately sized portions. Freeze by storing in zipper bags or sealed storage containers. The less air there is in the container, the better your chances are of safeguarding your foods from "freezer burn".

Whenever possible, prepare casseroles ahead of time in a pan or foil tin that can be easily frozen and kept in the freezer until a later date. Remember, however, that if you use a foil tin, you cannot use the microwave to defrost the casserole (unless, of course, you enjoy small pyrotechnic displays, the smell of plastic burning, and shopping for home appliances — like a new microwave). You can, however, remove the food from its metal container, slice it, and put individual slices on a microwave-safe plate.

And to all of the above, let me add just one more word of advice... have fun experimenting, because, after all, enjoying yourself is what it's all about!

Recipes For The Heart, Morsels For The Soul

CHAPTER FIFTEEN:
DINING OUT DEFENSIVELY... AND ENJOYABLY

Americans love eating out, and over the decades, it has even become a national pastime. An average American family eats one of every three meals outside the home, or almost 200 times a year. This translates to approximately 6 to 10 times per week. In fact, our population spends an average of more than $1,600.00 per person annually in restaurants. In the United States alone, the fast-food industry generates more than $60 billion a year. The statistics are exhausting, and that kind of spending can leave you low... on cash, that is, but not low on fat! Let's face it: anything that affects this much of our life should be done with a good basis of information.

An average American family eats one of every three meals outside the home... Anything that affects this much of our life should be done with a good basis of information.

Les always loved to say, "The world is full of good things to eat, and I'm going to enjoy everything I can." As far back as our early married days in Chicago, Les and I could be found every Saturday, between noon and 2:00 PM, at the counter of a local hot dog stand, consuming hot dog after hot dog. Les has always been a very slow eater, and always allowed his food ample time to digest. However, he never denied himself the pleasure of eating whatever he enjoyed. As with many people, what he did deny was the likelihood that a serious health problem would ever affect him. He certainly did not fit the profile of an obese "belly buster", and lacked the "beer-gut" you would normally associate with someone on the fast track toward a heart attack.

The question we must each ask ourselves is, "Am I on that same fast track, without even knowing it?"

Working your plan for eating out, as you do eating in, makes either location conducive to enjoyment, without compromising your healthy principles. But sticking with these principles when eating out can be a challenge, because those in the food business are quite proficient in the use of key phrases designed to market and sell to our *weaknesses*, not to keep us lean. It's up to us to learn to read between the lines. Once we do, we can discover that there is, indeed, such thing as a free lunch... fat-free, that is, and fabulous. And there's additional good news. More and more restaurants, fast-food and otherwise, have begun to respond to the consumer demand for good nutrition. They have analyzed the nutrition content of their food and have made their menus more user-friendly. Now, you can often choose your selections from a guide, so ask for nutrition information if you don't see it on the menu (or posted on the wall, as it is in some fast-food restaurants). Be informed about your choices, and bear in mind that the average fast-food meal yields about 1,500 calories! Use these calories wisely.

Many restaurants offer low-fat, low-cholesterol meals, and many label them with a symbol such as a heart ♥. When making your selection, it is important to understand how much fat, especially saturated fat, goes into the preparation of menu choices, including marinates and cookware lubricants. Portion size also can affect your menu selection.

Whether you're dining at the newest trendy uptown bistro, or grabbing a bite at the hamburger place up the street, follow these steps to success for "defensive dining out":

1. Plan to choose restaurants that offer a wide variety of healthful meals with which you are familiar. If you're a first-timer, don't go when you are starving!
2. Eating out offers socializing, so sit back, relax, enjoy the company, and savor the flavors... of other people.

3. Try to plan your order before you preview the menu, because pictures have a way of stimulating your appetite for selections you might otherwise not make.

4. Always drink a large glass of water before opening the menu. This should give you a feeling of "fullness" before you order, and before you get the urge to taste someone else's fried mushrooms.

5. Relish (veggie) trays are great for giving the mouth a good warm-up before the main meal. Be sure you "dip" in fat-free dressings.

6. If the portion is larger than needed, ask for that doggie bag as soon as the plate is put in front of you, and bring home Rover's dinner while it is still hot.

7. Tell your server exactly how you want your food prepared. Each restaurant wants you back, so speak up about your special needs and requests.

8. And remember, when faced with little choice but fast food, apply as many of your new "dining out" principles as possible. Eat based upon what you have learned. (*We'll have more on fast foods later.*)

More Tidbits For Your (Doggie) Bag Of Tricks

Still not convinced that I'm serious when I talk about "no-kidding, healthy cuisine while eating out"? Well, Les and I have discovered for ourselves that eating healthy when out is possible just about anywhere, including many national chain restaurants. In this section, I'll give you a few more tips and tricks to help you become a savvy diner.

Initially, when ordering, you may feel that you're being too particular. But you needn't be self-conscious, because many restaurants are becoming more used to the demands of health-conscious patrons. What's important is that you are confident in knowing your instructions are carefully followed.

The first thing to do is to rid your mind of how it might look to carry your own items into restaurants. After all, more and more people are doing it. In fact, you may actually be surprised at the number of restaurants that welcome the supplements you bring in. Many are glad that you feel comfortable enough to do so. They are happy when you are happy, because it means repeat business. Furthermore, in their conscious effort to accommodate their patrons, we have even seen some restaurants begin to offer similar healthy items. By the way, we *do* practice what we preach... Les has succeeded at this practice for years!

So how can *you* put your healthy principles into practice when eating out? Well, read on for examples of some seemingly difficult categories. You will surely be able to use your knowledge and imagination to apply the techniques more globally.

1. ***Let's begin with breakfast.*** Bring with you a spray bottle of nonfat butter substitute, such as I Can't Believe it's Not Butter™. If you like eggs, you will probably have to live with them in omelet, scrambled or similar form. Order *egg whites*, or *egg substitute*, and stress the importance of cooking them on a freshly clean and dry section of the grill, or, better yet, a separate clean and dry pan. Tell them not to use any butter, margarine, oil or cooking spray, and let them know that you're not worried about the egg product coming off of the pan smoothly. Hold your ground, or let them use only *your* fat-free spray, but be sure that they use very little. It is also important to instruct them to cook any added vegetables the same way: with absolutely no oil, and *no cooking spray* whatsoever.

What's that you say... you want hash browns on the side? No problem! The *same* clean, dry pan and *"no oil"* method of preparation holds true. It's cooking or frying with oil that is hazardous to your health. And guess what... just as with the omelet, you can add a couple of pump sprays to the potatoes, and voilá! You may not even be able to tell the difference!

2. *Moving through the day*, there are a number of other food choices that you might not think of as fitting into our "clean" (low-fat) and enjoyable repertoire. How about some pizza? Impossible, you say? Hey, you should know by now that once you've set your mind to healthy eating, very little is impossible.

♥ First, tell them to hold the cheese. You may not think much of pizza without cheese, but it's really not at all bad! Just be sure that you are getting only fresh vegetables that are not prepared with any oil. Stress to the order-taker that they carefully wipe all residual lubricant off the pan, so that it is *perfectly* dry. There may be some small unavoidable amount of oil or butter in the original bread dough, and we therefore recommend staying with *thin-crust* pizza. Basic pizza sauce will probably have very little or no fat. When it's done, you can give it a couple of shots from your trusty pump spray for moistness and taste.

♥ Don't forget, no cheese or meat products. (If you make pizza at home, you can use fat-free shredded mozzarella. Before placing it in the oven, it needs to be lightly, but evenly, misted with your non-fat butter spray, so that the cheese will stay moist and will melt. Otherwise, it will become toasty and dry on top.) Follow these tips, and you will have a great tasting veggie pizza that is extremely low in fat!

3. *One of the biggest problems for most people is finding a low-fat, "fast-food" lunch*. There is always salad with fat-free dressing, but by itself, that may not have an "everyday" appeal, especially when you're really hungry. An excellent popular choice is a Teriyaki bowl, typically including chicken, rice and vegetables. There are submarine sandwiches *without cheese* (turkey is usually the lowest in fat). Speaking of turkey sandwiches, you can have just about any grocery store deli counter make you one. Even Seven-Eleven and other convenience stores have joined the health watch, with vegetable and chicken bowls, fruit, turkey, and other items. In a pinch, you can even

eat the sliced turkey breast offered by barbecue restaurants. As always, leave off the mayo and "special sauces". Chicken breast is OK, as long as it's grilled, preferably on an *open* grill. Remember to check the nutrition guides, because as of this writing, one of the most well-known fast-food places (and one of the very few that uses an open grill), has about the highest fat content in their chicken sandwich. You also may have noticed that many restaurants offer veggie-burgers. Some are lower than others in fat, but again, be sure yours is cooked in a *dry* pan or open grill.

4. *This is for lovers of Chinese food.* You know by now that you will need to stay away from most buffet items. You can, however, order from the menu, and request everything to be prepared without any oil. Anything containing meat (except that which is completely lean, such as white meat chicken) needs to be avoided. Ask them what choices will have no fat or oil, and then be sure to have them *steam* your order. If there are items that must be stir-fried, be certain that they understand your needs when you instruct them not to use any oil. Water or chicken broth *with no oil* actually works well. Also specify that any gravy must be oil-free. Les always orders a gravy substitute, made with a little corn starch and garlic in boiling water (the mixture should be clear, not white). A small amount of soy sauce can also be added, but watch your sodium. Alternatively, chicken broth without any oil can also be used with the corn starch. It really works, and tastes fine! (By the way, it's advisable to request that no MSG be used in preparing your food, especially if you're sensitive to this additive.) For soups, Asian "Pho" is delicious and pretty clean when ordered without meat, and when the broth is oil-free. Rice noodles are usually best.

5. *Mexican restaurants are always popular, but typically don't make healthy meals as easy to spot.* This is a great example illustrating the need to "BYO". Just like everyone else, Les certainly likes to enjoy chips and salsa, so we are not embarrassed when we bring our own low-

fat, baked chips! (The salsa is usually fat-free, but stay away from the cheese dip.) One of our favorite entrées is the Fajita Platter. We are very specific when ordering chicken to be grilled totally dry (again, no sprays or other lubricants). The same goes for the accompanying vegetables. Also, the corn tortillas will usually be lower in fat than the flour tortillas, and avoid the refried beans and cheese. When you receive your order, you might use the fat-free spray butter to moisten it all up a bit, and even try adding a little fat-free Italian dressing to the chicken and vegetables for a great taste! (And if you like the flavor, a squeeze of fresh lime juice will add moisture and a little "zing".)

6. *As for Italian...* well, now we come to another American favorite. You may need to make a few changes in your preferences for this one, but you *can* succeed! For starters, bring your own fat-free spray butter, fat-free Italian salad dressing, and, if you like bread, you may also want to carry in your own fat-free spread. Go easy on the bread, however, because when combining it with pasta, your carbohydrates will really skyrocket. Obviously, we need to eliminate any appetizers that are fried or contain any oil, butter, margarine, whole milk, cream, or other fatty ingredients. Order your salad either with nonfat dressing or balsamic vinegar. The minestrone soup will often be reasonably low in fat, but be sure there is no cheese on top. The big change for some of you will be in the main course. Avoid meat fillings, and no more Alfredo sauce or anything else with a cream base. Have them cook your pasta without oil in the water (most decent restaurants can and will), and use tomato-based sauces with very little or no oil. Once again, a shot of that miracle butter substitute spray and fat-free Italian dressing will add moistness and great flavor to almost any Italian main dish.

7. *Now for a challenge: buffets!* But there's good news here, too. Les always loved the "all you can eat" buffets, and he still does. The difference now is that he makes proper choices. (Here's where the mind control and visualization techniques we spoke of earlier really do their

job!) Beware that some restaurants featuring buffets will simply not offer much of what you need. However, many of the larger and more modern places now do. You can, of course, chow down on vegetables from the salad bar, using nonfat dressings. Find out which soups are not cream-based and have very little or no oil. For your main course, choose only lean white-meat turkey or chicken breast without gravy. Low-fat fish is always an excellent choice, as long as it is not marinated with butter. (In addition to your fat-free spray butter, some fat-free soups are great for moistening.) Ask for your rolls without any butter. Find out which cooked vegetables do not have *any* butter in the water. Come equipped with your own toppings for baked potatoes, or you can even use fat-free ranch dressing! Jell-O or nonfat frozen yogurt is fine for dessert, but, sorry, none of those brownies or cream pies! If you are on the way to developing your attitude techniques, you'll be amazed at how much you can really enjoy this "healthy buffet", and many other meals!

Always An Alternative!

Here are a few substitution ideas to consider when dining at restaurants. Use your imagination and creativity to expand on these:

TRY REPLACING:	WITH:
All Salad Dressings	Any Fat-Free Dressing (Including Caesar)
Shrimp Bisque or Other Cream-Based or Oily Soups	Vegetable Soup (non-oil based)
Buffalo Chicken Wings	Grilled or Baked Chicken Strips Dipped in Fat-Free Ranch Dressing or Salsa
Egg Rolls	Steamed Dumplings
French Fries	Baked Potato Sticks with Rosemary
Fried Rice	Steamed Rice
Croissants	French Bread or Sliced Sourdough
Veal Parmigiana	Veal Marsala
Fried Seafood	Grilled or Broiled Seafood
Pastries	Fruit

Open Your Eyes
Before You Open Your Mouth

Here are some more "red flags" to watch for:

TEN "FWF" ("FILLED WITH FAT") CAUTION SIGNS:
1. Alfredo
2. Batter-dipped
3. Creamy
4. Crispy
5. Scalloped
6. Flaky
7. Tempura
8. Supreme
9. Super-sized
10. Au gratin

HIGH SODIUM WARNING WORDS:
☹ Smoked
☹ Pickled
☹ Bouillon
☹ Soy sauce
☹ Teriyaki
☹ Cured

When you're armed with information, along with your own low-fat condiments and seasonings, there's no reason that you can't enjoy eating out as much as you always have — without compromising your new healthy way of life!

CHAPTER SIXTEEN:
EAT, DRINK AND CHILL

lthough it is vitally important, you need to remember that eating "right" is not the only component of your health program. Proper exercise and stress control are also essential to optimize your odds. One without the others makes it less likely that you will maintain your life-long commitment to yourself. This is of particular importance to those of you who are sedentary for much of your day!

Just as with any other muscle, your heart needs to be kept "in shape". Any activity that gets your heart pounding, and your lungs really breathing, is music to your cardiovascular system's ears. (That would mean, in theory, that lovemaking could be considered as a workout! Oh, the sacrifices we must make for a healthy lifestyle...) In most cases, the average adult heart pumps about 65 beats per minute during sedentary intervals, but during intense aerobic exercise, might beat up to 200 times per minute. What that means is (as my mother always says): "If you don't move, you won't move!"

And it's not just my mom. Ask any doctor about exercise, and they will all agree about its invaluable benefits.

On the next page, you will find a little self-test to help you determine your activity level. Rate how well each statement describes your typical behavior by circling the appropriate number.

Eating right is vitally important, but please don't neglect the "work-out" and "chill-out" components of your total health program!

SCORING SYSTEM:	1=ALMOST ALWAYS			5=NEVER
I travel in an automobile, a bus, or a train when I need to go somewhere.	1 2	3	4	5
I choose the parking space closest to my destination.	1 2	3	4	5
I get off the bus at the stop closest to my destination.	1 2	3	4	5
I find efficient shortcuts when I walk.	1 2	3	4	5
I take the elevator down.	1 2	3	4	5
I take the elevator up.	1 2	3	4	5
I sit down during my breaks.	1 2	3	4	5
Between supper and bedtime, I watch television or read.	1 2	3	4	5
I choose to watch sports or other activities rather than participate in them.	1 2	3	4	5

Add the numbers you circled and rate yourself:

SCORE:

0 to 18: SUPER-SITTER; SPICE UP YOUR LIFE BY LOOKING FOR OPPORTUNITIES TO STAND AND MOVE!

19 to 36: MEDIUM MOVER; YOU ARE MOVING ABOUT, BUT THERE IS STILL ROOM TO GROW!

OVER 36: ACTIVITY ACE; YOU HAVE THE SPIRIT! WEIGHT MANAGEMENT SHOULD BE FAIRLY EASY!

Exercise Your Options

A common recommendation is to exercise at least three times a week, with your heart rate at 70% to 75% of its maximum for a full 30 minutes. Your maximum is figured by subtracting your age from the number 220.

Regular aerobic exercise can greatly reduce the risk of heart disease and heart attack. As long as you are moving, your heart is getting increased blood flow. Anything, however, is certainly better than nothing, as long as it is not causing an "out-of-shape" heart to be over-pushed. Again, be absolutely sure to obtain full clearance from your physician before beginning or increasing any exercise regimen.

As a side note, always maintain proper hydration, especially during exercise. Drink lots of water. In fact, there is beneficial value to drinking ample amounts of water throughout the day. The feeling of fullness can divert hunger and cravings, and keeping the body fluids recycled helps minimize lingering waste.

Walking has always been the movement of choice for many, particularly at the beginning of an exercise program. Some studies show that fast walkers (five miles per hour or more) actually burn twice as many calories as runners moving at the same speed. When the goal is life-long health, however, we are not out to break any Olympic records. So, when your doctor gives the thumbs-up, begin by putting one foot in front of the other and go. Start by going to work a little earlier, parking farther from the office, and taking the stairs instead of the elevator on a consistent basis. A regular exercise program maximizes energy while minimizing stress. It can improve physical *and emotional* well-being. My mother also says, "Moving the body moves the mind."

Relaxation: I Can't Stress It Enough!

This brings us to the topic of stress reduction. We all know that the feelings of stress can be very "distressing"! Emotional and physical stress both come from the way we respond to changes, or to issues which affect us throughout the day. Research has shown that unmanaged long-term stress weakens the immune system and is more likely to fuel illness. Writing about the various causes of stress could potentially take a book as large as *War and Peace*. So here's the "skinny" on stress management for a total sense of well-being.

Step one for stress management is to discover, or perhaps re-discover, an activity you truly enjoy. Then, as stated by a popular sport-shoe manufacturer, "Just do it." If you enjoy listening to music or books on tape, grab a head set and pedal, walk or run while combining the activity with exercise. This brings a positive connection to movement. If it's ballet, jazz or any dance that you enjoy, join a class and start moving. Try an activity that you have always wanted to do, or did when you were younger, and notice how this can become an instant stress reliever. You will notice that the mechanism is two-fold. First, you are taking your mind off of what ails you… your well deserved "escape" time, if you will. Second, the physical exertion increases production of endorphins, which build a positive attitude, and an overall healthy feeling. Later, after your session is over, it can also promote relaxation.

Step two is to participate in an enjoyable adult education course, and visualize this as a way to take leave from some of your daily sources of stress. Nurture this activity as a positive step toward improving your overall stress level (and keeping your brain active, alert, and "young"). The key word here is "enjoyable"; make your activity fun, and keep it as a regular routine. Many people also find meditation exercises can be a great relaxation outlet, and can promote more restful sleep.

Step three is to *always* stay conscious of your breathing. Breathe, breathe, breathe… *deeply!*

I hope these tips will get you started on your way to creating your own exercise routines and stress-busters. Do what works best for you, but do something. Eating right is vitally important, but please don't neglect the "workout" and "chill-out" components of your total health program!

IN CONCLUSION . . .

Thank you for letting me share our story, our passions, and our strong convictions about the importance of health. It is through our love of life that Les and I have learned the real importance of wellness. As with many of you, our road has not been an especially easy one. But though it has had some significant obstacles, each today has taught us more about tomorrow. And while trends come and go, we are certain that the desire for good health and longevity will be popular forever.

We've given you some of the tools to embrace these treasures in your own life. Please don't wait until the bomb hits. We encourage you to be wise and courageous enough to learn from others who have already experienced that wake-up call. Please, please realize and remember that in great part, health truly is in your own hands, by the recognized healthy choices that you make. Participate wholeheartedly in your health agenda, and enjoy living each new day!

RECIPES

I put together each of these recipes by analyzing all the ingredients and studying the availability of each product before including it in this book. Each one was tested for quick cooking time, ease of preparation, and enjoyable flavor for the entire family. To ensure my success in developing these low-fat recipes, I had Les and many other brave souls of various ages test each recipe. In fact, many have withstood the scrutiny of taste-testers for five years! Only those that elicited unanimous approval made the final cut to be included in this book. I can assure you, there were plenty that didn't make the grade, either because they were too difficult to prepare, or they inspired only a sympathetic (for the cook) comment such as, "This isn't too bad" from one or more of my gracious and willing taste testers.

In each of these recipes, nutrition information was determined based on the ingredients used. The fat contents were estimated by using the most current fat-gram information from the manufacturers' labels on products purchased both commercially and from retail grocery stores. Each recipe has less than one fat gram per serving. Increasing or decreasing certain ingredients in the preparation of foods (such as cooking sprays), can slightly alter the total fat content of the final dish. For example, nonfat cooking sprays are often used throughout these recipes. Bear in mind that sprays are essentially "oil in a can", and as of the date of this writing, spraying *for one-third of one second* is the label notation that allows most of them to actually be called "fat-free". Since that small amount may not cover your entire pan, one of the techniques we suggest is to use a clean, lint-proof paper towel or cloth to spread the scant recommended amount of spray evenly around the pan.

To keep these recipes fat-free or very low fat, stick closely to the precise ingredients listed (except for possible brand substitutions when necessary), especially those ingredients which affect the fat, cholesterol, and calorie contents. To eat healthfully, it is also important to maintain the indicated portion and serving sizes.

Have fun experimenting! Here's to your health... and a long and joyful life!

. . . APPETIZERS . . .

ARTICHOKE CHILI DIP

1   *14-ounce can artichoke hearts, drained and chopped*

1   *4-ounce can chopped green chili*

1   *cup fat-free mayonnaise*

1/4   *cup fat-free Parmesan cheese*
      Vegetable cooking spray

Preheat oven to 350 degrees.

Mix artichoke hearts, green chilis, cheese and mayonnaise into a bowl.

Spray an 8-inch round baking dish or quiche pan.

Add mixture to pan.

Bake uncovered for 30 minutes.

Serve warm with vegetables or fat-free crackers or rice cakes.

SERVES: 10
CALORIES: 106

Similar to the recipe at the right, but modified to please the palates of my Texas cooks. The green chiles really give it zing!

ARTICHOKE DIP

1   16-ounce container nonfat sour cream
6   tablespoons grated nonfat Parmesan cheese
2   scallions (green onions), finely chopped
1   teaspoon crushed garlic
1   14-ounce can artichoke hearts, rinsed,
    drained, and finely chopped
    Vegetable cooking spray

Preheat oven to 350 degrees.

Blend sour cream, Parmesan cheese, scallions, and garlic together in a bowl.

Mix until creamy.

Mix in artichokes.

Pour into a baking dish or quiche dish, lightly sprayed with cooking spray.

Bake 20~30 minutes or until lightly browned on top.

Serve warm. Use table crackers or flat bread for dipping.

SERVES: 10~12
CALORIES: 45

A great warm dip for any holiday occasion. Most guests think it tastes too rich and creamy to be fat-free.

BAKED CRABMEAT DIP

1	*6-ounce can white crab meat, packed in water*
1/2	*cup fat-free sour cream*
1/4	*cup fat-free mayonnaise*
2	*tablespoons minced onion*
2	*tablespoons fat-free Italian salad dressing*
1	*teaspoon dill*

Preheat oven to 350 degrees.

In a small bowl combine crab meat, sour cream, mayonnaise, minced onion, salad dressing and dill.

Pour the dip in a shallow baking dish or quiche dish.

Bake covered with aluminum foil for 40 minutes.

Serve warm.

You may want to cut out the end of a round bread loaf and serve the dip in the middle of the bread, with bread cubes, low-fat crackers or a flat bread or melba toast.

SERVES: 6~8
CALORIES: 90

Not only is this dip tasty, serving it in an edible bowl results in no left-overs (and fewer dishes)!

CRAB MOUSSE

1   8-ounce package light cream cheese, softened
1   pound imitation crab, ground up in the food
    processor
1/4 cup scallions, finely chopped
2   tablespoons fat-free Miracle Whip™
1   small jar cocktail sauce

Line a bowl with plastic wrap and mix all the
ingredients except the cocktail sauce together.
Form the mixture into a ball and place into the
center of the plastic wrap in the bowl.
Refrigerate at least one hour.
Unmold and pour cocktail sauce over the mousse
before serving.
Serve with low-fat crackers.

SERVES: 10~15
CALORIES: 65

OMEGA MAN

Shellfish is high in cholesterol, but low in saturated fats, and the omega-3 fatty acids actually help to reduce cholesterol levels in the body. How's that for an oxymoron!

CRAB STUFFED PORTOBELLO MUSHROOMS

3	Portobello mushrooms, washed and cleaned
1	cup chopped tomatoes
1	teaspoon minced garlic
1	teaspoon onion powder
2	tablespoons chopped cilantro
1	tablespoon Marsala cooking wine
1	8-ounce package crab meat, ground up in food processor
	Fat-free Italian salad dressing
	Vegetable cooking spray

Preheat oven to 375 degrees.

Wash and clean mushrooms.

Remove stems and reserve.

Chop the stems up and put the stems into a bowl, adding the chopped tomatoes, cooking wine, garlic, onion, and cilantro.

Mix well.

Spray the bottom of a shallow baking dish with cooking spray and add enough water to the dish to cover the bottom.

Lightly brush the tops and bottoms of the mushrooms with the Italian dressing and place in shallow baking dish.

Add the mixture to the mushrooms and top with crab.

Bake for 30-40 minutes.

SERVES: 2
CALORIES: 119

CRANBERRY FRUIT DIP

1   cup nonfat yogurt, vanilla or lemon
1   cup whole berry cranberry sauce
1/4   teaspoon cinnamon
1/8   teaspoon ground ginger

Combine ingredients and dip fresh fruits such as bananas, apples, kiwi and strawberries.

SERVES: 8
CALORIES: 35

Use cranberries year-round to add color, freshness, and a delightful fragrance to your dishes. Using ground ginger also adds an aromatic zest to your fresh vegetables.

CREAM CHEESE BITES

1   *8-ounce package fat-free cream cheese, soft ened*

1   *teaspoon basil*

1/2 *teaspoon garlic powder*

1   *teaspoon low-fat buttermilk*

1   *teaspoon dill*

Mix all the ingredients together with a fork.

Top with cucumber slices.

Spread on low fat table crackers, Melba rounds or cucumber slices.

SERVES: 10
CALORIES: 45

CREAMY SPINACH DIP

1   10-ounce package frozen chopped spinach,
    thawed, squeezed dry and strained
1   cup nonfat sour cream
2   scallions, cut into chunks
2   teaspoons dried dill weed
2~3 teaspoons lemon or lime juice

Process all ingredients in a food processor or
blender until smooth.

SERVES: 10
CALORIES: 60

This is a tangy varia-
tion on the spinach dip
we've all been served
at parties. Be sure to
drain the spinach well
to bring out all the
flavor.

EGGPLANT SPREAD

2   *medium eggplants (approximately 2 pounds)*
1   *tablespoon lemon juice*
2   *cloves garlic, peeled and chopped*
1   *tablespoon fresh dill, finely chopped*

Preheat oven to 375 degrees.

Poke several holes in each eggplant with a fork and place in a baking pan.

Bake for one hour or until soft. Remove from oven and allow to cool.

Cut eggplant in half and remove skin and seeds.

Place cooked eggplant in a blender or food processor.

Add remaining ingredients and blend until creamy.

Chill before serving.

Serve with low-fat table crackers.

SERVES: **6~8**
CALORIES: **41**

You can serve this with any meal using pita bread, low-fat crackers, or raw vegetables.
It is best to use fresh dill or parsley. Fortunately, most grocery stores now carry fresh herbs and spices.

When preparing other dishes with eggplant, try using chives, grated onion, garlic, oregano, or tarragon. Fresh herbs and spices will make each dish tasteful and flavorful while allowing you to cut down on sodium. The key nutrients in this spread are vitamin A, vitamin C, fiber, and iron.

FAT-FREE VEGGIE DIP

2	cups fat-free cottage cheese (16 ounces)
1	cup green pepper, seeded, finely chopped (2 medium)
2	tablespoons catsup
1	teaspoon celery seed
1	cup shredded carrots (2 medium)
1/4	cup minced onion
1	teaspoon lemon juice
1/2	teaspoon ground pepper

Combine all of the ingredients in the food processor or blender.

Mix until smooth.

Cover in bowl and refrigerate at least 2 hours before serving.

SERVES: 8~10
CALORIES: 78

I always make this for New Year's parties, and we all play "Guess the secret ingredient" (it's catsup).

FIESTA RANCH BEAN DIP

1   11-ounce package Fiesta Ranch Party Dip™
        mix
1   16-ounce can fat free refried beans
1/2   pint fat-free sour cream (8 ounces)
1   7-ounce can diced green chilies
1/2   cup fat-free cheddar cheese

Cream and mix all ingredients thoroughly.

Dip with baked chips or cut up fresh vegetables.

SERVES: 10
CALORIES: 20

This is a perennial hit at Super Bowl parties, which are a BIG tradition in Dallas, Texas.

FRUIT SALSA

3	medium Granny Smith apples
2	kiwis, peeled
2	cups hulled strawberries (10~12 medium sized)
1	orange
3	tablespoons brown sugar
4	tablespoons apple jelly

Peel, core, and slice apples.

Cut apples into quarters and blend in the food processor.

Peel and core strawberries and kiwis and cut up (by hand — not in the food processor).

Mix well (again, by hand).

Cut the orange in half and squeeze the orange juice from one half into the fruit mixture.

Scrape the zest off of the other orange half.

Add the brown sugar and apple jelly into a large bowl and combine with the fruit mixture.

Refrigerate and serve cold.

Can dip with baked cinnamon sugar crisps or cinnamon graham crackers.

The zest is the outside shaving from fruits such as oranges or lemons. Don't use the white part below the skin...bitter!

SERVES: 10

CALORIES: 51

REFRIED BEAN DIP

1	16-ounce can fat-free refried beans
1	4 1/2-ounce can chopped green chilies
1/2	teaspoon each, ground cumin and garlic powder
1/4	cup chopped cilantro leaves

Mix all ingredients in a bowl until blended.
Serve with baked chips.

SERVES: 10
CALORIES: 39

Tex-Mex recipes were my favorite to develop, and easily turn into family favorites.
Note: recipe is for dried cilantro. If using fresh, chop finely and use less.

PINWHEELS

10	*fat-free flour tortillas*
2	*8-ounce bars fat-free cream cheese, softened*
1	*green pepper, chopped*
1	*red pepper, chopped*
1	*bunch scallions, chopped*
1	*can chopped water chestnuts or chopped celery*
1	*package Hidden Valley Original Ranch™ Powder Dressing*

Mix all ingredients and spread on flour tortilla.

Roll up and refrigerate in waxed paper or Saran Wrap.

Cut into slices and serve when cold.

SERVES: 10

CALORIES: 35

SALMON SPREAD

1   small (6-ounce) can salmon, drained and strained

1   8-ounce package lite cream cheese

1   tablespoon lemon juice

2   teaspoons grated onion

3   tablespoons parsley flakes

2   tablespoons dill

Mix together the first four ingredients with a spoon until creamy.

Sprinkle in dill and parsley.

Line a cereal-sized bowl with plastic wrap and press mixture on plastic wrap into the bowl.

Refrigerate.

Unmold spread by turning bowl over onto the plate.

Serve with low-fat table crackers.

SERVES: 12

CALORIES: 24

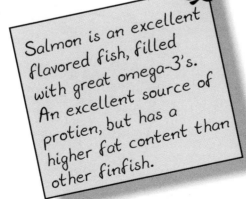

Salmon is an excellent flavored fish, filled with great omega-3's. An excellent source of protien, but has a higher fat content than other finfish.

SALMON LOG

1	small can salmon, drained
1	8-ounce package lite cream cheese
1	tablespoon lemon juice
2	teaspoons grated onion
3	tablespoons parsley flakes
	Parchment, wax paper, or plastic wrap

Mix together the first four ingredients until creamy.

Roll the mixture in the parsley flakes until well coated.

Wrap the log in parchment, wax paper, or plastic wrap.

Chill.

Serve cold with low fat crackers.

SERVES: 10~15
CALORIES: 52

Canned salmon can be eaten with the bones. They are tenderized, full-flavored, and offer terrific nutrition... A great way to get calcium!

SHRIMP MOUSSE

1   8-ounce bar fat-free cream cheese, softened
1   small can shrimp, drained and mashed
1   tablespoon minced onion or scallions
2   tablespoons fat-free mayonnaise
1   small jar cocktail sauce

Line a small bowl with plastic wrap.

Mix all of the ingredients except the cocktail sauce
into a ball.

Refrigerate at least one hour.

Pour cocktail sauce over before serving.

Serve with your choice of crackers (Wheat Thins™
are my personal favorite).

SERVES: 15~20
CALORIES: 38

Loaded with nature's nutrients of iron, calcium, zinc, and magnesium. Always buy seafood from a reputable source.

WONTON WRAPPERS

Wonton wrappers
Vegetable cooking spray
FILLERS (your choice):
   Chicken salad
   Cherry, blueberry, or apple pie fillings
   Tuna salad
   Egg- white egg salad

Preheat oven to 350 degrees.

Lightly spray a 6-muffin tin with cooking spray.

Mold a wonton skin inside each opening.

Lightly spray each skin with cooking spray.

Bake for 10~12 minutes. Do not overbake, as they will easily burn.

Remove shells from muffin pan and let cool.

Fill only within 20 minutes of serving or the skins will become soggy.

SERVES:	6
CALORIES:	30

Wontons are thin, paper-like skins, made from flour and water, found in the produce section of most grocery stores. After baking these (don't let them burn), you can fill them with just about anything. The wonton becomes an edible dish. Fill them at the last minute so they do not get soggy.

. . . BEVERAGES & CONDIMENTS . . .

BANANA-BERRY DRINK

1   *banana, peeled*
3/4 *cup skim milk*
1/2 *cup raspberry flavored nonfat yogurt*
1   *package artificial sweetener*

Mash banana with fork.

Add yogurt and milk.

Frappê in blender.

Add sweetener.

For variety, use various flavors of yogurt.

SERVES: 4
CALORIES: 82

Bananas are an excellent source of carbohydrate with fiber and vitamin C. Bananas are terrific for potassium, too. Honey may be substituted for sweetener.

ICED COFFEE

1/4   cup crushed ice or 4 ice cubes

1/4   cup nonfat chocolate frozen yogurt

2   tablespoons water

1   tablespoon Farm Rich™ fat-free non-dairy creamer

1   tablespoon sugar

1   teaspoon instant coffee

Process all ingredients in blender until smooth.

SERVES: 2
CALORIES: 87

CELEBRATION PUNCH

12   ounces raspberry cranberry juice

6   ounces orange juice

2   tablespoons lime juice

1   liter bottle club soda

Combine and enjoy!

SERVES: 6
CALORIES: 27

FRUIT SMOOTHIE

1   12-ounce container frozen apple juice concen-
    trate
2   cups skim milk
2   cups fresh or frozen fruits (bananas and
    strawberries work great), not thawed
6   ice cubes (if using fresh fruit)

Place all ingredients in the blender and blend until
smooth, creamy and frosty.

SERVES: 4
CALORIES: 63

Extracts add a terrific flavor to any smoothie. I would recommend Almond, Coconut or Vanilla. Try to serve your smoothie with a straw, as it makes the flavor last longer. Top the glass with a wedge of fresh fruit!

FETTUCINE ALFREDO SAUCE

1   15-ounce can evaporated skim milk
1/2   cup fat-free grated Parmesan cheese
1   chicken bouillon cube
2   tablespoons white cooking wine (optional)
2   tablespoons chopped fresh parsley
       Generous dash of ground nutmeg
       Generous dash of ground white pepper

In a saucepan, combine milk and cheese.

Slowly bring to a boil over medium heat, stirring often.

Add bouillon, pepper, nutmeg, and wine.

Simmer until mixture becomes thick.

Remove from heat.

Add to cooked fettuccine noodles and toss.

Sprinkle with parsley.

SERVES: 4
CALORIES: 105

EASY SALSA

2	*tablespoons onion, chopped*
1	*medium tomato, chopped (1 cup)*
1	*small jalapeño pepper, seeded and chopped*
1/2	*cup fresh cilantro, chopped*
1/4	*teaspoon sugar*
1/2	*teaspoon cumin*
2	*tablespoons lime juice*

Mix all ingredients together and blend in the food processor.

Add salt and pepper to taste.

SERVES: 6~8
CALORIES: 33

SOUTHWESTERN V-8 REFRESHER

1	*5 1/2-ounce can of V-8™*
1	*tablespoon lime juice*
1/8	*teaspoon chili powder*
	Dash of hot pepper sauce

Blend and drink.....hot,hot,hot

SERVES: 8
CALORIES: 29

SEAFOOD MARINADE

2 cups lite tamari sauce

1/2 cup unsweetened pineapple juice

2 cloves garlic, chopped

1/4 teaspoon ground ginger

1/8 teaspoon crushed red peppers

Mix together and marinate seafood up to two hours.

SERVES: 2

CALORIES: 35

SWEETENED SEAFOOD MARINADE

1/2   cup lite soy sauce

1   teaspoon garlic powder

1   cup diet 7-Up™

Mix together and pour over seafood.

Marinate up to two hours.

Will cover 2 filets.

SERVES: 4

CALORIES: 50

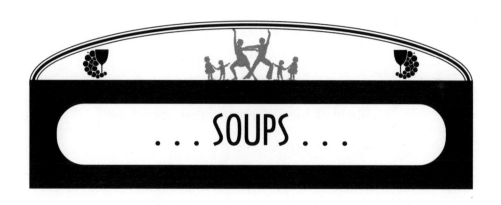

. . . SOUPS . . .

GAZPACHO

1   16-ounce can low sodium, fat-free beef broth

1   30-ounce can plum tomatoes, diced

1   12-ounce can tomato juice

1   6-ounce can vegetable juice

2   tablespoons crushed garlic

1   each: red, yellow, and green sweet peppers, chopped

1   bunch green onions, chopped

3   stalks celery, finely chopped

2   tablespoons Worcestershire sauce

1   bunch fresh cilantro, chopped

Blend all ingredients together, mixing well.

Serve cold with non-fat yogurt.

SERVES: 6

CALORIES: 103

MUSHROOM BARLEY SOUP

4   *onions, diced or put through the food processor*

12   *stalks of celery, finely sliced*

2   *tablespoons crushed garlic*

6   *cups water*

6   *cups nonfat chicken broth*

2   *cups barley*

4   *pounds fresh mushrooms*
       Dash pepper
       Dash dill
       Vegetable cooking spray

Spray a large 3~4 quart soup pot with vegetable spray.

Add onion and celery; cook, stirring often, until softened (about 10 minutes).

Add garlic and cook 2 minutes longer.

Add broth, water, pepper, barley and dill.

Reduce heat and lower heat to cook, uncovered, for 1 1/2 hours.

Add mushrooms and cook for another 20 minutes.

SERVES: **8~10**

CALORIES: **119**

POTATO MUSHROOM SOUP

2	cups dried baby lima beans
2	quarts cold water
1	large onion, diced
2	stalks celery, diced
1	tablespoon crushed garlic
2	14 1/2-ounce cans low-fat chicken or beef broth
2	carrots, diced
2	cups mushrooms, sliced
4	large potatoes, peeled and sliced
1/4	teaspoon pepper
	Vegetable cooking spray

Sort and wash beans and soak overnight.

Drain and rinse.

Spray the bottom of a 4-quart soup pot with vegetable cooking spray.

Sauté onions, celery, and garlic for 8~9 minutes, or until tender.

Add broth, water, beans, carrots, mushrooms, and pepper.

Simmer gently, stirring occasionally, for 1 hour.

Add potatoes and cook for 1/2 to 1 more hour, or until beans and potatoes are tender.

SERVES:	8~10
CALORIES:	92

SEAFOOD SOUP

1/2 pound each of 2 varieties seafood (shrimp, crab, halibut), cut into small pieces

1 8-ounce can Mexican style stewed tomatoes

1 large onion, finely chopped

1 tablespoon crushed garlic

2 medium potatoes, cut into pieces

1 cup white wine or cooking wine

1 cup water

Fresh cilantro

Dash of salt and pepper

Vegetable cooking spray

Peel and boil the potatoes.

In a skillet sprayed with cooking spray, sauté the onions and garlic for 3~4 minutes.

Add the tomatoes (with the liquid), wine, and water.

Pour the mixture into a soup pot.

Add the potatoes to the pot.

Add seasoning and seafood to the mixture.

Stew for 1 hour.

SERVES: 4
CALORIES: 90

TACO BEAN SOUP

2	*4-ounce cooked chicken breasts, cut into small pieces*
1	*16-ounce can. fat-free refried beans (blend in food processor if creamy texture is desired)*
2	**cups chunky salsa (any degree of heat desired)**
2	**cups corn, drained (if using frozen, package needs to be thawed)**
1	**cup onions, finely chopped or put through the food processor**
2	**cups water**
1/3	**teaspoon chili powder**
1/4	**teaspoon cumin**
1	**tablespoon cilantro, finely chopped**

Combine all of the ingredients, except the cilantro.

Heat in a large stock pot for about 10 minutes.

Top with fat-free cheddar cheese and fresh cilantro.

Serve hot with baked tortilla chips on the top of the bowl.

SERVES: 6
CALORIES: 112

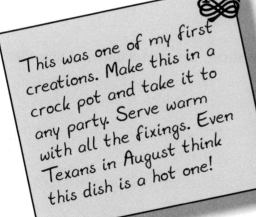

This was one of my first creations. Make this in a crock pot and take it to any party. Serve warm with all the fixings. Even Texans in August think this dish is a hot one!

TORTILLA TURKEY SOUP

1   package ground white meat turkey
2   6-ounce cans reduced-sodium nonfat chicken broth
1   16-ounce jar thick and chunky salsa
2   cups frozen corn, thawed and drained
1   tablespoon lime juice
3   tablespoons fresh cilantro
or
1 1/2 tablespoon dried cilantro
1/2 cup chopped onion
     Baked tortilla chips
     Nonfat cheddar cheese

Pour half of the chicken broth into a 12-inch skillet and heat.

Add the ground turkey and brown over medium heat for 7~10 minutes, stirring and chopping the meat into small pieces.

Add the remaining chicken broth, salsa, corn, chopped onion, and lime juice.

Bring to a boil and simmer for 10 minutes. (If the broth is too thick, add 1/2 cup water.)

Add fresh cilantro.

Top with baked tortilla chips and nonfat cheddar cheese.

Serve warm.

SERVES: 8
CALORIES: 112

. . . SALADS . . .

ASPARAGUS SALAD

2	pounds fresh asparagus, trimmed
or	
2	10-ounce packages frozen asparagus spears
1/4	cup balsamic vinegar
1	tablespoon sugar
1	teaspoon crushed garlic
3	cups torn mixed greens
2	green onions, sliced (1/4 cup)
2	hard-boiled egg whites, chopped
	Parsley

Cook the fresh asparagus spears in a saucepan in a small amount of boiling water for 8-10 minutes (or until crisp and tender), or cook frozen asparagus according to package directions.

Remove asparagus from the boiling water, reserving 2 tablespoons of liquid.

Dip ends into cold water.

Rinse with cold water and drain well.

Combine reserved liquid, vinegar, sugar, and garlic in a small bowl.

Place asparagus in a shallow dish and pour vinegar mixture over.

Cover and chill for 1 hour.

Place salad greens on a plate and arrange asparagus on top of the greens.

Top with green onions, egg whites and garnish with parsley.

Drizzle reserved vinegar mixture over salad.

SERVES: 6
CALORIES: 54

Asparagus has a great deal of foliate, which protects our blood vessels. Is best purchased in late winter and early spring. The tips are the most tender, so buy ones that are strong throughout the entire stalk.

AMBROSIA

1	*20-ounce can pineapple chunks in juice, drained*
1	*11-ounce can mandarin orange segments, drained*
1	*banana, peeled & sliced*
1 1/2	*cups seedless grapes*
1	*cup miniature marshmallows*
1	*8-ounce carton vanilla fat-free yogurt*

Combine pineapple, oranges, banana, grapes, and marshmallows.

Fold in yogurt.

Chill.

SERVES:	6~8
CALORIES:	162

CARROT SALAD

1	*cup nonfat mayonnaise*
2	*tablespoons vinegar*
4	*carrots, peeled and grated*

Mix the mayonnaise and vinegar together in a bowl.

Combine with the carrots.

Cover and refrigerate overnight.

SERVES:	4
CALORIES:	33

CAESAR SALAD

1   *large head dark romaine lettuce*

1   *teaspoon crushed garlic*

1   *teaspoon Worcestershire sauce*

1/4 *cup fresh squeezed lemon juice*

1/4 *cup grated nonfat Parmesan cheese*

1   *egg white.*

     Dash of pepper

     Olive oil or vegetable cooking spray

Wash lettuce and pat dry.

Lightly spray the leaves with the vegetable spray.

In a small bowl, whisk together Worcestershire sauce, garlic, lemon juice, and egg white.

Pour the dressing over the salad and toss well.

Sprinkle with Parmesan cheese and pepper.

SERVES: **4**
CALORIES: **40**

CARROT & JICAMA SALAD

1/2   *pound baby carrots*

1/2   *pound jicama, peeled*

1/4   *cup lemon juice*

2   *tablespoons fat-free Italian salad dressing*

1/2   *teaspoon crushed garlic*

1/2   *teaspoon chili powder*

      Dash of pepper

In a glass bowl with a tight-fitting lid or a clear plastic bag, mix all of the ingredients except the carrots and jicama.

Set aside.

Cut the jicama into strips and slice the carrots.

Pour the mixture over the carrots and jicama, coating well.

Marinate the vegetables in the refrigerator for at least 2 hours.

Stir well and drain before serving.

SERVES: **4**

CALORIES: **35**

Jicama is a Mexican potato. Though it is tough to peel, it's well worth the effort. Acts as a great veggie for dipping.

CHICKEN SALAD

1   cup fat-free mayonnaise or salad dressing

1   tablespoon lemon juice

1   tablespoon soy sauce

1/2 teaspoon celery salt

3   cups cooked skinless, boneless chicken breast, chopped

1   cup celery, chopped

1   can sliced water chestnuts, drained

1   pound seedless green grapes

1   large can mandarin oranges, drained

6   hard-boiled egg whites, chopped

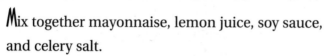

Mix together mayonnaise, lemon juice, soy sauce, and celery salt.

Toss other ingredients into mayonnaise mixture.

Place in refrigerator overnight so flavors will blend.

SERVES: 4
CALORIES: 136

CHICKEN TACO SALAD

2	*boneless skinless chicken breasts (3/4 pound), cubed*
1/2	*cup salsa*
3	*cups shredded lettuce*
1	*15-ounce can kidney beans, drained and rinsed*
1/2	*cup chopped tomato*
1	*cup green onions-chopped*
1	*8-ounce package fat-free cheddar cheese*
3	*cups baked tortilla chips*
	Vegetable cooking spray

Spray a skillet with the cooking spray.

Brown the cubed chicken in a hot skillet on medium high 5~7 minutes, until chicken is white and tender.

Reduce heat and stir in salsa.

Simmer 5~7 minutes.

Remove from stove.

Using a large salad-type bowl, layer the lettuce, beans, chicken and tomatoes.

Top with cheese and green onions.

SERVES:	4~6
CALORIES:	140

CRANBERRY GELATIN

1   *16-ounce can jellied cranberry sauce*

1   *8-ounce can crushed pineapple, drained (save liquid)*

2   *small packages sugar-free lemon Jell-O™*

1   *small package sugar-free cranberry or raspberry Jell-O*

2   *cups boiling water*

1   *cup pineapple juice with water added to equal 2 cups total*

1   *half-pint carton fat-free sour cream*

Dissolve Jell-O with 2 cups of boiling water.

Beat in all of the other ingredients except the crushed pineapple.

Put Jell-O mixture in a bowl to partially set in the refrigerator.

When it has partially set (about two hours), fold in the pineapple and mix well.

Pour into a Jell-O mold and refrigerate until firm.

SERVES: **8**

CALORIES: **160**

FAT-FREE POTATO SALAD

4	*large potatoes*
3	*tablespoons Dijon mustard*
2	*tablespoons prepared mustard*
4	*dill pickles, finely chopped*
2	*teaspoons garlic salt*
2	*teaspoons pepper*
2	*teaspoons paprika*
4	*tablespoons dill pickle juice*
1/2	*cup chopped onion*
4	*eggs, hard boiled (use egg whites only) & chopped*
1 1/2	*cup fat-free mayonnaise*
1/4	*cup horseradish (optional for extra spicy)*

Preheat oven to 350 degrees.

Bake potatoes until tender (approximately 1 1/2 hours).

Scoop out and mash.

Place mashed potatoes into a bowl, add remaining ingredients and mix well.

Top with paprika.

Let set in the refrigerator 2~3 hours.

If eggs crack when boiled, add a little vinegar to the water to seal the cracks.

SERVES: 4~6

CALORIES: 109

FRUIT JELL-O MOLD

2   *cups boiling water*

1   *8-ounce package cranberry flavor gelatin*

1 1/2 *cups cold ginger ale (sugar free or diet, if*
     desired)

2   *cups red or green seedless grapes, halved*

1   *11-ounce can mandarin orange segments,*
     drained
     Fresh mint (optional)
     Vegetable cooking spray

Pour boiling water into gelatin, stirring for 2 minutes.

Stir in cold ginger ale until completely dissolved.

Refrigerate about 1 hour, or until thickened and partially set (a knife drawn through leaves an impression).

Stir in fruit.

Spray a 5-cup mold with vegetable spray.

Spoon mixture into mold and refrigerate 4 hours, or completely firm.

Unmold onto serving platter.

Garnish with fresh mint or strawberries in the center if desired.

SERVES: **6~8**

CALORIES: **56**

FROG-EYE PASTA SALAD

3/4   cup sugar

2   tablespoons flour

1/4   teaspoon salt

1 3/4   cups pineapple juice

1   cup egg substitute

1   tablespoon lemon juice

1   package Acini de Pepe™ pasta

3   11-ounce cans mandarin oranges, drained

3   20-ounce cans pineapple, crushed and drained

1   9-ounce carton non-dairy whipped topping, light

1   cup miniature marshmallows

Combine sugar, flour, and salt into a small pan.

Gradually stir in pineapple juice and eggs.

Cook over medium heat, stirring constantly, until thickened.

Add lemon juice.

Cool mixture to room temperature.

Cook pasta according to package directions.

Drain and rinse well.

Cool at room temperature.

Combine egg mixture and cooked pasta.

Mix lightly but thoroughly.

Refrigerate overnight in an airtight container.

Add remaining ingredients, mixing lightly.

Keep salad refrigerated until served.

May be stored in the refrigerator up to one week.

SERVES: 25
CALORIES: 115

This dish gets its name by the fact that the Acini De Pepe pasta reminded my friend Irene of frog's eyes. Fortunately they do not taste like frogs' eyes..or legs. Remember: This recipe involves preparation over two days, but is well worth the time and effort.

MINTED RICE FRUIT SALAD

1	cup pineapple juice
1/3	cup water
1	cup uncooked instant rice
1	11-ounce can mandarin oranges, drained
1	8-ounce can crushed pineapple
1/2	cup chopped and peeled cucumber
1	small red onion, chopped
3	tablespoons fresh mint, chopped

Combine juice and water in medium saucepan.

Bring to a boil and stir in rice.

Remove from heat, cover, and let stand for 10 minutes.

Stir together rice, drained mandarin oranges, undrained pineapple, cucumber, onion, and mint.

Toss in a bowl.

Chill for 1 hour.

Serve cold.

SERVES: 4~6
CALORIES: 106

TACO SALAD BAKED SHELL

1   *large fat-free flour tortilla*
     Nonfat vegetable cooking spray or I Can't
     Believe It's Not Butter™ spray

Preheat oven to 450 degrees.

Place a medium-sized glass bowl upside down on a cookie sheet and lightly spray the outside of the bowl with the cooking spray.

Quickly dip the flour tortilla in warm water to soften, and spray with cooking spray.

Place the tortilla over the bowl and bake in the preheated oven for 5 minutes, or until lightly browned and firm.

Carefully lift the tortilla off the bowl and place the shell on its bottom on the cookie sheet.

Return to the oven and bake for 2~3 more minutes, or until crisp.

Cool at room temperature and fill with Taco Salad.

Pre-made shells may be stored in an airtight container for up to one week.

SERVES: 1

CALORIES: 156

VEGETABLE SALAD MOLD

1	*4-ounce package lemon Jell-O™ (use sugar-free if desired)*
1	*cup boiling water*
3/4	*cup cold water*
2	*tablespoons cider vinegar*
1	*teaspoon dill*
1/4	*cup green pepper, finely chopped*
2	*teaspoons Spanish onion, grated*
1	*teaspoon crushed garlic*
1	*cup chopped cucumber*
1	*cup chopped tomatoes*
	Vegetable cooking spray
	Dash ground pepper

Pour the Jell-O™ in a medium sized bowl.

Add boiling water and stir until dissolved.

Stir in cold water.

Add green peppers, vinegar, garlic, dill, pepper, and tomatoes.

Chill about 1 1/2 hours, or until thickened.

Fold in the cucumbers and onions.

Spray a 1-quart mold with cooking spray.

Pour the entire mixture into the mold.

Refrigerate until firm (approx. 4 hours).

SERVES:	**6**
CALORIES:	**60**

Recipes For The Heart, Morsels For The Soul

VEGGIE TORTILLA SALAD

1   cup salsa

1   can fat-free refried beans

3   cups shredded lettuce

1   15-ounce can kidney beans, drained and
     rinsed (optional)

1   cup chopped tomato

1   cup chopped green onions

1   8-ounce package fat-free cheddar cheese

3   cups baked tortilla chips

1   teaspoon garlic powder
     Fresh cilantro

In a large plate or deep bowl, mix the refried beans
with the salsa and garlic powder.

Blend until creamy.

Put salsa bean mixture in the center of the plate.

Sprinkle shredded lettuce around the outside of
the bean mixture.

Top the lettuce with chopped tomatoes, chopped
onions and kidney beans.

Sprinkle salad with cheddar cheese.

Round off the outer layer with baked tortilla
chips.

Sprinkle fresh cilantro onto the entire salad.

SERVES: 8
CALORIES: 120

...MAIN COURSES...

APPLE VEGETABLE PITAS

1/4   *cup apple, chopped, peeled and dipped in lemon juice*

1/4   *chopped or grated carrot (1 small)*

1   *tablespoon dried dill*

1/4   *cup chopped cucumber, seeded*

2   *tablespoons fat-free mayonnaise or plain non-fat yogurt (may adjust to desired consistency, but you want the filling to be thick, not runny)*

1   *pita bread*

In a bowl, mix the ingredients together (you can substitute or add any vegetables).

Slice open one end of the pita bread and fill the pocket with the mixture.

Wrap in plastic wrap.

SERVES: 4

CALORIES: 20

This is a great new spin on the ole sandwich idea. It's a great blend of fruits and vegetables, which are a wonderful source of carbohydrates with a new twist of "between the slices" Pita bread.

BARBECUE CHICKEN PIZZA

1   large Boboli™ pizza crust

3   boneless, skinless chicken breasts

2   cups barbecue sauce

2   cups veggies (red and green peppers, mush-
      rooms or onions, your choice), chopped

1   8-ounce package fat-free mozzarella cheese,
      grated
      Butter-flavored cooking spray

Preheat oven to 400 degrees.

Bake or broil chicken and cut into chunks.

Spoon barbecue sauce evenly over the pizza crust.

Add the chopped veggies and sprinkle the cheese to cover the top.

Add two squirts of butter-flavored cooking spray and bake for 12~15 minutes or until the cheese is melted.

Remove from the oven and slice.

Serve hot.

SERVES: 8

CALORIES: 297

Inspired by my cousin (and favorite cheer-leader), Marilyn Boskind, this dish raises eyebrows at first glance, but one taste, and you're hooked!

BAKED HALIBUT

2   *pounds halibut or any other fish steak (4-6 fillets)*

1   *cup onions (1 onion), thinly sliced*

2   *cups fresh mushrooms, thinly sliced*

1/2 *cup chopped tomatoes (2 small)*

1/4 *cup green bell peppers (1 pepper), chopped*

1/2 *cup low-sodium, low-fat chicken broth*

3   *tablespoons chopped pimiento*

2   *tablespoons fresh lemon juice*

1   *teaspoon fresh chopped dill*

1   *lemon, sliced into wedges*
     Vegetable cooking spray

Preheat oven to 350 degrees.

Lightly spray a covered baking dish with the vegetable spray.

Rinse fish and pat dry with paper towels.

Arrange the onion slices on the bottom on the dish.

Place fish on top and set aside.

In a separate bowl, combine the mushrooms, tomatoes, bell peppers, and pimiento.

Mix well and arrange on top of the fish.

In a small bowl, mix together the chicken broth, lemon juice, and dill.

Pour over the fish and vegetable mixture.

Cover and bake 25~30 minutes or until the fish flakes easily when tested with a fork.

Garnish with fresh lemon wedges.

SERVES: 8
CALORIES: 116

Halibut is a very low-fat fish. It is available year round, easy to prepare and very tender. You can cook this fish by steaming, baking, poaching; almost any way will taste great.

BAKED CORN FLAKE CHICKEN NUGGETS

2   *pounds boneless, skinless chicken breasts (3 breasts)*

3   *cups corn flakes cereal or corn flake crumbs*

1/8   *teaspoon pepper*

1/2   *cup fat-free Parmesan cheese*

1   *cup skim milk*

1/4   *cup egg substitute*

       Vegetable cooking spray

Pre-heat oven to 350 degrees.

Rinse the chicken breasts under cold water.

Pat dry with a paper towel.

Cut each chicken breast into 2-inch strips.

Mix corn flakes, pepper, and Parmesan cheese in a plastic bag (if using corn flakes cereal, crush with a rolling pin).

Pour one cup skim milk and egg substitute into shallow dish and mix well.

Dip the chicken pieces into the milk mixture and shake in the bag containing the corn flakes.

Coat a cookie sheet with vegetable spray.

Line chicken strips on the cookie sheet.

Bake the chicken nuggets for 35-45 minutes, turning every 15 minutes.

SERVES: 4

CALORIES: 213

Do not overbake or they will taste, to quote my daughter Jackie, "like hockey pucks!" You can either buy pre-crushed corn flake crumbs or, if using cereal, put the cereal in a plastic bag, seal it up, visualize your boss, and pound away!

CHICKEN AND VEGETABLES IN A CREAM SAUCE

4	*skinless, boneless chicken breasts*
1	*teaspoon crushed garlic*
1	*10 3/4-ounce can reduced fat cream of mushroom soup*
1	*cup skim milk*
1	*teaspoon lemon juice*
1/4	*teaspoon dried basil*
1	*16-ounce bag frozen vegetables (your choice), thawed and drained*
	Vegetable cooking spray

Spray a skillet with 1-2 sprays of cooking spray and heat for 1 minute.

Cook chicken for 5~7 minutes or until it turns white with a little browning color. Set aside.

In a small pan, simmer soup, milk, lemon juice, basil, garlic, and vegetables, stirring often.

Add the vegetable mixture and the chicken to the skillet with the soup mixture.

Cover and cook over a low heat for 10~15 minutes or until chicken is done and tender.

SERVES: 4
CALORIES: 66

CHICKEN KABOBS

4   *skinless, boneless chicken breasts*

2   *green peppers, cut into bite-sized chunks*

1   *large onion, cut into bite-sized chunks*

1   *zucchini, sliced*

1   *tomato, cut into bite-sized chunks*

2   *cups Teriyaki sauce*

      Kabob sticks

Preheat oven to 350 degrees.

On each kabob stick, skewer alternating chunks of chicken, peppers, onions, zucchini and tomatoes.

Place in a marinating and cooking pan.

Combine 1 cup Teriyaki sauce with 1 cup water and pour over the kabobs.

Cover and bake the kabobs for 40 minutes, basting with the Teriyaki sauce at 20 minutes.

Remove the foil for the last 5~7 minutes.

Serve warm over a bed of couscous and chopped tomatoes or rice.

SERVES: **4**
CALORIES: **122**

CHICKEN FAJITA PITA

3	*boneless and skinless chicken breasts (2 pounds), cooked*
1	*package fajita seasoning mix*
1	*cup shredded lettuce*
1	*tomato-sliced*
1	*cup fat-free grated cheddar cheese*
1	*pita bread*

Cut chicken breast into strips.

Sprinkle the meat with fajita seasoning.

Slice one side of the pita bread to form a pocket.

Fill the bread with the chicken, shredded lettuce, tomatoes, and cheddar cheese.

SERVES: 8

CALORIES: 109

This was one of the first recipes I developed. I now find packaged grilled fajita chicken strips in the grocery stores, , so if you want to cut down on your work load, buy these.
We have even seen rattle snake fajitas on a restaurant menu. Not for me, but if it sounds good to you, go for it!

FAJITAS

6   *4-ounce skinless, boneless chicken breasts,*
     cooked (may be grilled) -about 3 cups

1   *package frozen whole sweet corn, thawed*

2   *Spanish red onions, sliced*

2   *green bell peppers, sliced*

1   *red bell pepper, sliced*

1   *8-ounce jar mild picante sauce*

1   *bunch fresh cilantro, chopped*

1   *package fat-free flour tortillas*

For condiments:

1   *package or container of fat-free or light*
     sour cream, and shredded cheddar cheese

Cut grilled chicken breasts into strips.

In a large skillet on top of the stove, add one inch of water to steam the onions, peppers, and corn to soften for 10 minutes.

Add 1/2 cup picante sauce.

Add chicken and fresh cilantro.

Cover and let simmer 20 minutes.

To *make individual fajitas:*

Fill each flour tortilla with the chicken and vegetable mixture.

Add cheese and sour cream, and extra picante sauce if desired.

SERVES: 8
CALORIES: 190

CHICKEN ROLLS

1   *package fat-free flour tortillas*
2   *skinless, boneless chicken breasts*
or
1   *can white meat chicken*
1   *head of romaine lettuce*
2   *tablespoons fat-free mayonnaise*
1   *pinch of pepper*
1   *bunch alfalfa sprouts*

Boil, bake, or broil the chicken breasts until they are not pink when cut into.

Chop the chicken breasts in the food processor or blend very finely.

In a separate bowl add the chicken, mayonnaise, pepper, and alfalfa, mixing well.

Spread a very thin layer of the mixture on each flour tortilla.

Top with a leaf of lettuce.

Roll the tortilla up and wrap in waxed paper.

Chill in the refrigerator for 1 hour.

Slice into 1-inch pieces and skewer with toothpicks to retain shape.

SERVES: 8~12
CALORIES: 40

I had developed this recipe before the concept of wraps became popular. When using the fat-free flour tortillas, be sure to wrap them up in either waxed paper, plastic wrap or foil after they are made, so they will not dry out before you eat 'em.

FIREHOUSE CHICKEN

1	*8-ounce bottle fat-free Catalina™ dressing*
1	*envelope onion soup / recipe mix*
1	*8-ounce jar apricot preserves (all fruit style)*
2	*pounds chicken breasts, skinned*

Preheat oven to 350 degrees.

Mix first 3 ingredients together.

Spread enough of the mixture to cover bottom of baking dish.

Layer chicken over mixture.

Cover chicken with remaining mixture.

Cover and bake for 30 minutes.

Uncover and bake for an additional 30 minutes.

Serve over rice.

SERVES: 8
CALORIES: 249

700 million people suffer from protein deficiency world-wide. A food is considered a good source of protein if it contains at least 25 grams of this nutrient. This entire dish has 60 grams of protein, from the chicken, and is bursting with flavor.

CHICKEN WRAP UP

1   *box instant rice*
4   *chicken breasts (2 cups), grilled and cut up*
1/2 *cup fat-free ranch dressing*
1   *cup shredded lettuce*
     Flour tortillas

Cook rice according to the package directions.

Mix chicken with the ranch dressing and rice.

Spoon mixture onto the flour tortilla and add lettuce.

Roll up.

SERVES: 4
CALORIES: 93

This is an especially fast, easy dish that does a great job of satisfying your family's craving for moist, flavorful foods. Just don't get between Les and a plate of these! It could be dangerous!

EGGPLANT PARMESAN

1	large eggplant, peeled
2	egg whites, beaten
or	
1/2	cup egg substitute
1/4	cup skim milk
1	27 1/2-ounce jar lite spaghetti sauce
2	cups bread crumbs, crushed
1	8-ounce package fat-free mozzarella cheese
4	teaspoons fat-free Parmesan cheese

Preheat oven to 350 degrees.

Slice eggplant into thin slices.

In a shallow dish, mix the egg whites and skim milk.

Dip the eggplant slices into the egg mixture.

Pour the bread crumbs into a separate shallow dish and dip the eggplant into the bread crumbs.

Line the bottom of a baking dish with 1/2 of the jar of spaghetti sauce.

Line the eggplant in rows in the casserole dish.

Add the rest of the sauce.

Sprinkle with Parmesan cheese and top with the mozzarella cheese.

Cover and bake for 45 minutes.

SERVES: 4~6
CALORIES: 220

Eggplant is naturally high in vitamins A & C, fiber, and iron. If extra season- ing is required, try to stick with fresh herbs such as oregano and basil, rather than salt.

VEGGIE CHEESE ITALIAN

1	red pepper, finely chopped
1	zucchini, peeled and finely chopped
1	onion, finely chopped
2	tomatoes, finely chopped
1	27 1/2-ounce jar lite spaghetti sauce
1	package lasagna noodles
1	8-ounce package nonfat mozzarella cheese
2	cups nonfat plain yogurt
2	cups nonfat cottage cheese

Preheat oven to 350 degrees.

Boil noodles per package directions and drain.

Pour one inch of water in a skillet and steam all of the vegetables (except the tomatoes) in the water until soft and tender (5~7 minutes).

Remove from the skillet.

Pour the spaghetti sauce in the bottom of an oven safe casserole dish.

Add layers of noodles and steamed vegetables.

In a separate bowl, combine the yogurt and cottage cheese, mixing well.

Add the yogurt mixture to the next layer.

Top with sliced tomatoes, and sprinkle with cheese.

Cover and bake for 45 minutes.

SERVES: 8
CALORIES: 165

Recently, when I taught a class and prepared this dish, I discovered a "no-boiling" lasagna noodle that was just fantastic. If you use these noodles, just layer them with other ingredients like the prepared noodles. Easy!

VEGETABLE LASAGNA

1	16-ounce package fat-free lasagna noodles
2	15-ounce containers fat-free ricotta cheese
1	8-ounce container fat-free cottage cheese
1/2	cup fat-free egg substitute
1	large zucchini, peeled
1	medium onion, chopped
2	carrots, grated
1	package mushrooms, sliced
1	27 1/2-ounce jar fat-free spaghetti sauce
1	10 1/2-ounce can fat-free tomato soup
or	
1	14 1/2-ounce can diced tomatoes
1	6-ounce can tomato paste (optional)
1	8-ounce package shredded fat-free mozzarella cheese
1/4	cup skim milk
4	teaspoons fat-free Parmesan cheese Vegetable cooking spray

Preheat oven to 375 degrees.

Cut up all vegetables and sauté in pan on stovetop with vegetable cooking spray.

Cook lasagna noodles according to package directions.

In a large bowl, combine Ricotta cheese, cottage cheese, egg substitute, skim milk, and 1/4 cup mozzarella cheese.

In a medium-sized bowl, combine spaghetti sauce, tomato paste, and tomato soup.

Layer all ingredients, beginning with sauce and ending with lasagna noodles.

Top with remaining mozzarella cheese and sprinkle with Parmesan cheese.

Cover and bake for 45 minutes.

SERVES:	8~10
CALORIES:	315

LASAGNA CHICKEN NOODLE ROLL-UPS

10	*cooked lasagna noodles*
8	*ounces boneless skinless chicken breasts, cut into chunks*
2	*cups finely chopped broccoli*
1/2	*cup fat-free cottage or Ricotta cheese*
2	*egg whites or 1/4 cup egg substitute*
1/2	*teaspoon minced fresh chives*
1/4	*teaspoon ground black pepper*
1	*medium tomato, seeded and chopped, or 1 can chopped tomatoes*
1	*jar low-fat spaghetti sauce.*

Preheat oven to 375 degrees.

Cook lasagna noodles according to package directions, omitting salt.

Drain and rinse well under cold water.

Place in a single layer on aluminum foil.

Spray large nonstick skillet with cooking spray.

Add chicken and cook over medium heat until no longer pink.

Stir in broccoli and cook until broccoli is crisp-tender (about 3 minutes).

Cool.

Chop chicken finely.

Combine cottage cheese, egg substitute or egg whites, and pepper, and stir into chicken mixture.

Spread a generous 1/3 cup filling over each lasagna noodle.

Roll up noodles, starting at the short end.

Place filled rolls, seam side down, in a 10x8-inch baking dish.

Pour sauce over filled rolls.

Cover dish with foil and bake for 30-35 minutes.

Top with chopped tomato.

SERVES:	8~10
CALORIES:	125

MANICOTTI

1   *8-ounce box manicotti (14 shells)*

1   *15-ounce carton fat-free ricotta cheese*

1/2 *cup egg substitute*

or

2   *egg whites, beaten*

1/4 *cup fat-free Parmesan cheese*

1   *8-ounce package grated fat-free mozzarella cheese*

1/4 *teaspoon crushed garlic*

1/4 *teaspoon parsley, dried*

1/2 *teaspoon oregano, dried*

1/4 *teaspoon black pepper*

1   *27 1/2-ounce jar lite spaghetti sauce*

1   *14 1/2-ounce can chopped tomatoes*

1   *package frozen chopped spinach-thawed and drained (optional)*

Preheat oven to 375 degrees.

Cook pasta according to the package.

Drain and rinse well. Cool on a single layer of foil.

In a large bowl, stir together the ricotta cheese, parsley, pepper, crushed garlic, egg substitute, and oregano.

Spread into cooled pasta tubes.

Combine the spaghetti sauce with the tomatoes.

Spread a thin layer of sauce on the bottom of a 13x9x2-inch glass baking dish.

Arrange the pasta shells in a single layer over the sauce.

Add spinach to the shells.

Pour the remaining sauce over the pasta shells.

Cover with foil and bake 40 minutes.

Remove the foil and bake 5~7 minutes more.

Top with cheese and bake uncovered until the cheese melts.

SERVES: 6~8
CALORIES: 120

This was the very first dish my dear friend Wendy Geisler prepared for my family after we returned home after Les's angiplasty. Boy, was it terrific-and healthy too!

MEXICAN PIZZA

Fat-free or low-fat flour tortillas
1   *can fat free re-fried beans*
1   *package fat free cheddar cheese*
1   *can diced chili peppers/tomatoes*

Preheat oven to 375 degrees.

Spray pizza pan with cooking spray.

Layer:

- Flour tortilla
- Re-fried beans (thin layer)
- Diced chili peppers/tomatoes

Repeat layers.

Top with cheddar cheese.

Bake 12-15 minutes or until cheese has melted and all ingredients are softened.

Slice into segments like a pizza.

Serve hot.

SERVES: 2~4
CALORIES: 178

My true claim to fame. This was the first recipe I went public on a Local Texas broadcast TV show called "Good Morning Texas." Debra Duncan, a well-known TV host, loved it..you will too!

... Main Courses ...

HASH BROWN BOTTOM CASEROLE

1   34-ounce package frozen hash browns, thawed

1   cup egg substitute

2   cups mixed vegetables- carrots, broccoli, peppers (or any favorite combination) fresh or thawed- ground in the food processor

1   12-ounce package fat-free grated cheddar cheese

1/2 cup skim milk

1   teaspoon fresh dill

1   sliced tomato

    Dash pepper

    Vegetable cooking spray

Preheat oven to 375 degrees.

Spray the bottom and sides of a casserole dish with cooking spray.

Line the bottom of the dish with uncooked hash brown potatoes.

Add the vegetables to the next layer.

Sprinkle dill and pepper.

Pour the egg substitute and skim milk throughout the casserole.

Top with cheddar cheese.

Bake covered for 45 minutes, or until hash browns are golden brown.

Uncover, top with sliced tomatoes and heat 10~12 extra minutes.

Serve warm.

SERVES: 4~5
CALORIES: 120

This can be done with browned turkey sausage, bacon or meat. It can be served for breakfast, lunch or dinner. Les adds catsup....you know, potatoes. It is optional, depending on your taste!

PASTA MARZETTI

1   *pound ground turkey or ground chicken*

2   *onions, finely chopped*

1   *large (16-ounce) bag of your choice of frozen*
     vegetables (broccoli, carrots, cauliflower)

1   *large (14 1/2-ounce) can stewed tomatoes*

1   *26-ounce jar low-fat spaghetti sauce*

1   *can water (using the spaghetti sauce can)*

1   *4-ounce package dry macaroni noodles*
     Mrs. Dash™ seasoning
     Vegetable cooking spray

Sauté onion in the cooking spray in a large skillet.

Add turkey or chicken and Mrs. Dash™.

Cook until brown.

Add vegetables.

Continue cooking until vegetables are tender.

Add spaghetti sauce and water to the mixture.

Cook the noodles in a separate pan according to package directions.

Drain, rinse well, and add to the skillet.

Cover and simmer for 12~15 minutes, stirring frequently.

SERVES: 6~8
CALORIES: 118

This was passed down and revised from cousin Marilyn Boskind. It's easy, tasty and has its roots in Toledo, Ohio.

SALMON PATTIES

1   6-ounce can water-packed red salmon
1   small boiled potato, mashed or chopped in the
     food processor
1   medium onion, finely chopped (the food
     processor is great for this task)
2   egg whites
or
1/2 cup egg substitute
2   cups corn flake crumbs, crushed
     Dash of pepper
     Vegetable cooking spray

Preheat oven to 375 degrees.

Spray a large skillet with vegetable cooking spray
and sauté the onions for 5~7 minutes.

Drain liquid from the salmon.

Mix mashed potato, beaten eggs, and onion with
the salmon. (Note: If you are using a food processor
to do this, be careful not to process the salmon too
long, or your patties will come out heavy.)

Form into patties.

Pour the corn flakes into a plastic bag and crush.

Pour the corn flake crumbs into a shallow dish and
dip the salmon patties into the corn flakes.

Spray a cookie sheet with vegetable cooking spray.

Arrange patties on the cookie sheet, about 1 inch
apart, and bake for 12~15 minutes.

Turn patties and bake until brown on the other side.

Serve warm.

SERVES: 6
CALORIES: 85

Salmon, being a cold water fish, is considered a fattier fish, but has almost 4 grams of Omega-3's and can aid in lowering blood fats, especially triglycerides. Don't worry about canned salmon having bones. They are ground and tenderized and offer nutrition.

SHRIMP PITA POCKET

12	*ounces small shrimp, peeled and cooked*
2	*cups coleslaw mixture (pre-shredded)*
1/2	*cup fat-free Catalina ™ dressing*

In a bowl, combine shrimp, coleslaw mixture and dressing.

Fill the pita pocket with the shrimp mixture.

SERVES: 4

CALORIES: 200

Shrimp has a small amount of Omega-3's fish oils, but is also low in saturated fats. Added to pita with Catalina dressing makes for a great lunch on the go dish. You can now find pre-shredded lettuce and coleslaw packages in all grocery stores.

SEAFOOD RICE CREOLE

1/2   *cup chopped onions*

1   *cup green peppers, diced*

1/2   *cup mushrooms, diced*

1/4   *cup Marsala cooking wine*

1/4   *teaspoon crushed garlic*

2   *tablespoons basil (dried or fresh)*

1/8   *teaspoon red pepper flakes*

1/8   *tablespoon balsamic vinegar*

1   *tablespoon low-sodium tomato paste*

1/4   *cup fat-free, low-sodium chicken broth*

1   *pound of fresh fillet seafood (shrimp, crab, catfish), cut into cubes*

8   *ounces instant rice*

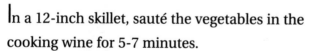

In a 12-inch skillet, sauté the vegetables in the cooking wine for 5-7 minutes.

Add spices, vinegar, tomato paste and broth.

Simmer 20 minutes.

Add seafood and simmer 10-15 additional minutes.

Cook rice according to directions.

Pour Creole sauce over rice.

SERVES: **4**

CALORIES: **84**

HOLIDAY STRATA

MAIN COURSES

1   loaf white or whole grain bread
1   12-ounce package fat-free cheddar cheese
1   cup egg substitute
1   16-ounce package frozen vegetable mixture-
     your choice (thawed)
I   6-ounce can crabmeat (optional), ground up
     in the food processor
2   tablespoons dill
     Dash of garlic
     Dash of paprika
     Vegetable cooking spray

Preheat oven to 375 degrees.

Cut the crust off the bread slices.

Spray a rectangle 9x13-inch casserole dish with the cooking spray.

Lay the slices of bread on the bottom of the baking dish, forming the first layer.

Top with vegetables and half the cheese.

Repeat layers.

In a separate bowl mix the crabmeat, egg substitute and garlic together.

Pour the mixture evenly over the casserole dish.

Top with dill and paprika.

Bake for 45~50 minutes.

SERVES: **10~12**
CALORIES: **48**

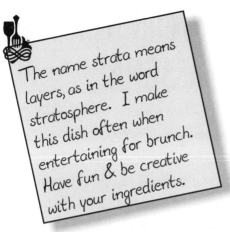

The name strata means layers, as in the word stratosphere. I make this dish often when entertaining for brunch. Have fun & be creative with your ingredients.

SHRIMP CREOLE

1	pound cooked shrimp (small frozen or fresh peeled)
1/2	cup diced bell pepper
1/2	cup chopped onion
1	teaspoon crushed garlic
2	8-ounce cans tomato sauce
1/8	teaspoon black pepper
1/4	teaspoon chili powder
4	cups cooked white rice
	Vegetable cooking spray

Spray skillet with cooking spray.

Add vegetables and sauté over medium heat.

Add garlic, tomato sauce, and seasonings, and simmer for 15 minutes.

Add shrimp and cook 10 minutes more.

Serve over cooked rice.

SERVES: 6

CALORIES: 200

SOUTHWESTERN TEX-MEX LASAGNA

4	cups cooked chicken breasts, cut up into small pieces (four 4-ounce chicken breasts)
1	10-ounce package lasagna noodles
1	16-ounce carton non-fat cottage cheese
1	10-ounce can diced tomatoes and green chilies
1	teaspoon chopped parsley
1/2	cup egg substitute
1	green pepper, chopped finely
1	red onion, chopped finely
1/2	teaspoon crushed garlic
1	10-ounce can enchilada sauce (mild)
1/2	teaspoon chili powder
1	teaspoon ground cumin
1/4	teaspoon black pepper
1	11-ounce can Italian tomato soup
1	8-ounce package fat-free shredded cheddar cheese
1	jar picante sauce (mild)
	Vegetable cooking spray

Preheat oven to 375 degrees.

Cook noodles according to the package.

Drain and set aside.

Mix together egg substitute, cottage cheese, parsley, tomatoes and diced green chilies.

Spray a large skillet with vegetable cooking spray.

Set aside.

Add onions, peppers and garlic. Cook over medium heat until the vegetables are tender (5-10 minutes).

Stir in tomatoes soup, enchilada sauce, chili powder, cumin, black pepper, and diced chicken breasts.

Bring to a slow boil.

Reduce heat and simmer, uncovered, 10-12 minutes, stirring often.

Spray a 13x9x2-inch baking pan.

Put lasagna noodles on the bottom.

Add half the cheese mixture.

Add the sauce mixture and chicken.

Layer all of the ingredients, ending with picante sauce and cheddar cheese.

Cover with foil and bake 60 minutes.

Let cool.

SERVES: 6~8
CALORIES: 120

SPAGHETTI PIE

1	*package spaghetti (3~4 cups)*
1/3	*cup grated nonfat Parmesan cheese*
2	*egg whites (well beaten) or 1/4 cup egg substitute*
2	*cups nonfat cottage or Ricotta cheese*
1	*pound lean ground turkey*
1	*cup chopped onion*
1	*cup chopped green pepper*
1	*8-ounce can tomatoes, diced*
1	*teaspoon oregano, crushed*
1	*teaspoon garlic powder*
1	*cup fat-free grated mozzarella cheese*
	Vegetable cooking spray (butter flavored) or non-fat butter substitute

Preheat oven to 350 degrees.

Cook the spaghetti according to the package directions and drain.

Spray butter flavored spray onto hot spaghetti.

Stir Parmesan cheese and egg whites or egg substitute into the spaghetti.

Spray the bottom of a deep dish pie plate.

Form spaghetti mixture into a "crust", forming the bottom layer.

Spread the cottage cheese on top of the spaghetti crust.

Spray a skillet and sauté onions and green peppers until tender.

Place vegetables in a separate bowl.

Add the ground turkey to the skillet and brown.

Drain off fat.

Stir in undrained tomatoes, oregano, and garlic powder.

Heat through.

Pour meat and vegetable mixture over spaghetti crust.

Bake uncovered for 45 minutes.

Top with mozzarella cheese.

Bake 5 minutes longer until cheese melts.

SERVES: 6
CALORIES: 110

See Chapter 14 for tips on making "Perfect Pasta."

SPINACH EGGPLANT PARMESAN

1	medium size eggplant
1	26-ounce jar pasta sauce
1	15-ounce can tomato sauce
2	cups fat-free or baked croutons
1	package frozen chopped spinach, thawed and drained
1/2	teaspoon oregano
1	package fat-free mozzarella cheese, grated
	Fat-free Parmesan cheese
	Egg substitute (equivalent to 1 egg)

Preheat oven to 350 degrees.

Peel the eggplant and slice into thin slices.

Pour half of the pasta sauce and half of the tomato sauce into the bottom of a rectangular baking pan.

Pour 2 cups of egg substitute into a shallow dish.

Put 2 cups of croutons into the food processor and crush finely.

Add the oregano to the crouton mixture.

Dip each eggplant slice into the egg substitute and then into the crouton mixture, covering completely.

Line the bottom of the baking dish with the coated eggplant slices, overlapping the slices to close large gaps.

Lay the spinach on the top of the eggplant mixture and cover with the remaining sauces.

Top with the grated mozzarella cheese.

Sprinkle with Parmesan cheese.

Bake covered for 45 minutes and uncovered for 10 minutes, or until lightly browned.

Serve warm.

SERVES: 6~8
CALORIES: 160

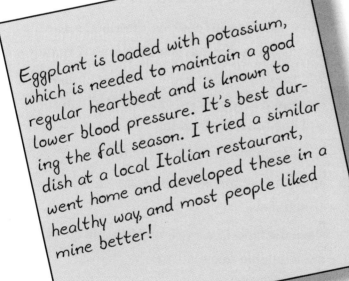

Eggplant is loaded with potassium, which is needed to maintain a good regular heartbeat and is known to lower blood pressure. It's best during the fall season. I tried a similar dish at a local Italian restaurant, went home and developed these in a healthy way, and most people liked mine better!

SUCCULENT SALMON

3	*pounds salmon filet*
2	*large onions, put through the food processor*
1	*teaspoon crushed garlic*
1	*bunch fresh basil, ground up in food processor*
1	*cup Marsala cooking wine*
1	*can chopped tomatoes*
1	*can veggie Italian soup*
1	*can water (use soup can)*
	Vegetable cooking spray

Preheat oven to 375 degrees.

Spray a skillet with cooking spray and sauté the onions and garlic over low heat for 5~7 minutes.

Add the cooking wine, the chopped basil, the entire can of tomatoes, one can of Italian soup, and one full can of water.

Simmer on low heat for 5~7 minutes.

Rinse the salmon with cold water, and cut into 4-inch filets.

Place the filets in a casserole dish and cover with the vegetable sauce mixture.

Bake for 35 minutes.

Cover with foil and bake another 20 minutes.

Serve hot.

SERVES: **6**
CALORIES: **105**

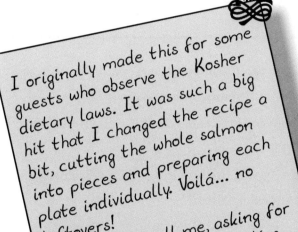

I originally made this for some guests who observe the Kosher dietary laws. It was such a big hit that I changed the recipe a bit, cutting the whole salmon into pieces and preparing each plate individually. Voilá... no leftovers!
Many people call me, asking for this recipe for dinner parties.

SWEET AND SOUR TURKEY MEATBALLS

1~2 *pounds ground white turkey breast*
2   *bottles chili sauce*
2   *bottles water (use chili sauce bottle)*
2   *tablespoons grape jelly*
1/4   *teaspoon garlic powder*
1/4   *cup ground bread crumbs*
2   *tablespoons egg substitute*

Combine the meat with the egg substitute, bread crumbs, and seasonings, mixing well.

Combine the chili sauce, water, and grape jelly in a deep pot.

Roll the turkey mixture into small balls and gently place into the sauce.

Bring the sauce to a boil, then reduce to medium heat and simmer for 1 1/2 hours, mixing often.

Serve warm over wide noodles or pasta.

SERVES: 10
CALORIES: 110

I recommend that you modify this recipe with what I call my "Boiling Your Balls" technique, which makes my male chef friends cringe. It makes these meat balls moist and tender. After you follow the directions in forming the meat balls, drop them into a large pot of boiling water. Boil the meatballs for 45 minutes to 1 hour. This cooks the meat and boils out the fat, while making the meat balls very tender.

After you have boiled the meat balls, drain out the water and put the meat balls in a fresh pot of the sauce. This allows the meat balls to cook in the sauce, allowing the flavors to cook in, while the fat has been pre-cooked out. This is a great technique for adding flavor, while reducing fat.

This recipe was passed down from my Aunt Rose, who was famous for her sauce. The meatballs need to simmer for a very long time so that they will cook through and through, as there is no skillet browning. You can also cook the meatballs in your favorite marinara sauce to pour on top of spaghetti.

TURKEY MEAT LOAF

2	pounds lean ground turkey
1/2	carton egg substitute
1	teaspoon onion powder
1/2	cup bread crumbs
1	teaspoon garlic powder
1/2	cup fat free Catalina ™ salad dressing
1/4	teaspoon barbecue sauce
1 1/2	cup frozen mixed vegetables, thawed, drained, and ground fine in the food processor
	Dash of Grey Poupon™ mustard

Preheat oven to 375 degrees.

Combine all ingredients.

Mix well with meat and put into a meat loaf pan (a double-drip meat loaf pan is preferred).

Bake for 45 minutes, or until well done.

SERVES:	**6~8**
CALORIES:	**224**

There are several types of meat loaf pans available, but I recommend the two-pan type. The meat loaf sits in a pan with a strainer of holes on the bottom. This allows the fat to drain out into a separate pan, while leaving in all of the flavor. You can find this type of pan in stores that sell cookware.

TEX-MEX BEAN CASSEROLE

6	*fat-free flour tortillas*
1	*16-ounce can kidney beans, drained*
1	*yellow onion, chopped*
1/8	*teaspoon pepper*
1	*teaspoon crushed garlic*
1	*tablespoon oregano*
1	*cup fat-free, low sodium chicken broth*
1	*15-ounce can diced tomatoes*
1	*8-ounce can tomato paste*
1	*12-ounce can Rotel ™ tomatoes*
1	*16-ounce can fat-free refried beans*
1	*8-ounce package non-fat grated mozzarella cheese*
1	*package baked tortilla chips*
	Vegetable cooking spray

Preheat oven to 375 degrees.

In a saucepan, combine beans, onion, garlic, seasonings, and chicken broth.

Stir and heat.

Add diced tomatoes, tomato paste, Rotel tomatoes, and refried beans.

Simmer 5-7 minutes over low heat.

Spray the bottom of an 11 x 7 glass baking dish.

Tear each of the flour tortillas into small pieces, and line the bottom of the dish with the tortilla pieces.

Pour 1/2 of the bean sauce mixture over the flour tortillas and 1/2 of the mozzarella cheese, and top with the remaining bean mixture and the rest of the cheese.

(The very top layer is a combination of the rest of the cheese and crumbled up tortilla chips.)

Bake uncovered for 30 minutes.

SERVES: 8
CALORIES: 170

TORTILLA CASSEROLE

1	package 6-inch corn tortillas
1	4-ounce can chopped green chili peppers, drained
1	10-ounce can Rotel™ tomatoes, chopped (preserve the juices)
2	chopped green onions (scallions)
1	medium red bell pepper, chopped
2	medium tomatoes, diced (or 1 can diced tomatoes)
2	cups skim milk
1/2	cup egg substitute
1	8-ounce package non-fat cheddar cheese, shredded
1	bunch fresh cilantro, chopped
	Vegetable cooking spray

Preheat oven to 325 degrees.

Coat a 9-inch glass baking dish with the cooking spray.

Tear the corn tortillas into small bite-size pieces.

Place a layer of tortilla pieces on the bottom of the dish.

Add a layer of the green onions, bell peppers, and half of the Rotel tomatoes and green chilies.

Repeat the vegetable layers, followed by another layer of corn tortillas, and then add half the cheese.

In a separate dish, mix the egg substitute and skim milk together.

Add the juices from the can of Rotel tomatoes.

Pour the skim milk-tomato juice mixture and the remaining Rotel tomatoes over the casserole.

Top with cheddar cheese and diced tomatoes.

Sprinkle fresh cilantro on top.

Bake covered for 30~40 minutes.

Serve warm with baked Tostitos™ and/or picante sauce on the side.

SERVES: 8
CALORIES: 75

TUNA PATTIES

2   6 1/2-ounce cans red salmon or water-packed
        tuna
1   large boiled potato (boil approximately 40
        minutes)
1   medium onion
1/2   cup egg substitute
2   cups corn flake crumbs
1/4   cup fat-free Miracle Whip™
1/2   teaspoon Spike™ seasoning
1/2   cup skim milk
        Dash pepper
        Vegetable cooking spray

Preheat oven to 375 degrees.

Spray cookie sheet and a 10-inch skillet with cooking spray.

Sauté onion in the skillet.

Drain liquid from salmon or tuna.

Peel and mash the potato with fork.

Mix with tuna.

Add eggs, onion, and Spike, mixing well.

Add skim milk.

Put entire mixture in blender and pureé.

Add Miracle Whip to the tuna mixture and mix well.

Make into 4-inch round patties and dip into corn flakes.

Place the patties on sprayed cookie sheet and bake 12 minutes.

Turn and bake another 10 minutes.

SERVES: 8

CALORIES: 79

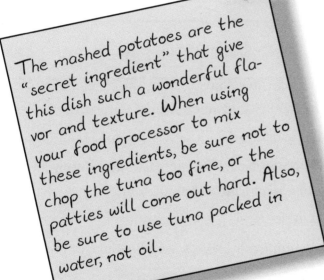

The mashed potatoes are the "secret ingredient" that give this dish such a wonderful flavor and texture. When using your food processor to mix these ingredients, be sure not to chop the tuna too fine, or the patties will come out hard. Also, be sure to use tuna packed in water, not oil.

TURKEY SLOPPY JOES

1	*Boil' n' Bag white rice*
1	*pound ground white meat turkey*
1	*green or red pepper, chopped*
1	*4-ounce can tomato paste*
1	*15-ounce can tomato sauce*
1	*package sloppy joe seasoning mix*
1	*teaspoon crushed garlic*
	Lite hamburger buns or English muffins
	Vegetable cooking spray

Prepare rice according to package.

Spray vegetable cooking spray on skillet and brown turkey and green pepper until tender.

Add crushed garlic.

Add tomato sauce, tomato paste, and sloppy joe seasoning and simmer 8-10 minutes.

Fold in rice.

Heat completely and serve on lite buns or English muffins.

SERVES:	**6**
CALORIES:	**100**

Ground turkey used to be a hard sell, but my recipes are always a hit, because these preparation methods preserve the moist flavor. And if you're wondering, "Is this turkey pretty low in fat?", the answer is Yes...8 ounces of white meat lean ground turkey has only 8 grams of fat.

TURKEY STUFFED CABBAGE

1	*head green cabbage (about 2 pounds) for 18~20 cabbage rolls*
1	*pound ground white-meat turkey breast*
2	*14 1/2-ounce cans crushed tomatoes*
2	*12-ounce bottles chili sauce*
2	*tablespoons grape jelly*
2	*medium onions, finely chopped*
1	*cup mushrooms, finely chopped*
1	*teaspoon dried parsley*
1	*teaspoon crushed garlic*
	Dash of pepper
	Vegetable cooking spray

Preheat oven to 350 degrees.

Remove the core from the cabbage and place in a large pot of boiling water.

Cover and boil for five minutes.

Remove from heat and let cabbage soak in the covered pot for 15~20 minutes, or until the leaves are wilted.

Drain and cool until easy to touch.

Peel off about 20 leaves that are tender and set aside.

Spray a large skillet with cooking spray and brown the turkey meat.

Add onions and garlic and sauté until clear and tender.

Add mushrooms and remaining seasonings and sauté until tender.

SAUCE:

Pour the chili sauce into a separate sauce pan.

Add two chili sauce bottles (24 ounces) of water.

Add the grape jelly and simmer 12-15 minutes.

In the center of each leaf, spoon in one tablespoon of the turkey mixture.

Add a little sauce to each cabbage roll.

Fold two sides of the leaf inward, and roll up.

Continue to fill each leaf until all of the meat is used up.

Coat the bottom of a 9x13- inch casserole dish with the sauce and place the cabbage rolls, seam side down, in the dish.

Cover the entire batch of cabbage rolls with the remaining sauce.

Cover and bake for 25~35 minutes.

This recipe was developed with the help of my brother-in-law, Larry Weinstein. We combined his love for creating stuffed cabbage meals with my enthusiasm for ground turkey. The sauce was inspired by my Aunt Rose from Toledo, who is famous for her chocolate chip cookies.

| SERVES: | 8 |
| CALORIES: | 91 |

TURKEY STUFFED GREEN PEPPERS

4	*medium-sized green peppers*
1	*pound lean white-meat ground turkey*
1/4	*cup crushed bread crumbs*
1/4	*cup egg substitute*
1	*pound instant white rice*
1	*12-ounce bottle chili sauce*
1	*27 1/2-ounce jar lite spaghetti sauce*
1/4	*teaspoon crushed garlic*

In a mixing bowl, combine the ground turkey with the egg beaters, bread crumbs and crushed garlic. Mix well and set aside.

Hollow out the inside of each green pepper and rinse well in cold water.

In a large pot, combine the spaghetti sauce with the chili sauce, and add one chili sauce bottle of water.

Add the rice to the turkey mixture and fill each green pepper with the mixture.

Bring the sauce to a boil and add the green peppers.

Boil the mixture for 1-1/2 hours while the pot is simmering to cook the meat and rice thoroughly. Serve warm.

SERVES: 6

CALORIES: 220

Tip:
You can make any extra meat into cocktail meatballs. Guests love them!

TUSCANY ITALIAN CHICKEN

1   *pound boneless, skinless chicken breasts, cut into cubes*
1   *tablespoon minced garlic*
1   *14 1/2-ounce can diced tomatoes (with juices) or 3 diced fresh tomatoes*
1   *cup chicken broth*
1   *14 1/2-ounce can whole new potatoes, strained, rinsed, and cubed*
1   *26-ounce jar Mediterranean style pasta sauce*
1   *14 1/2-ounce can cut green beans, strained and rinsed*
1   *medium bell pepper, diced*
1   *teaspoon basil*
    Dash pepper

In a 12-inch skillet, sauté chicken and garlic in chicken broth until the chicken is browned.

Add cut up potatoes, bell peppers, and diced tomatoes.

Continue to cook, stirring frequently.

Add the pasta sauce, basil, and green beans, and bring to a boil.

Reduce heat to medium, cover and simmer for 35 minutes, or until chicken is thoroughly cooked and tender.

SERVES: 6
CALORIES: 107

Tip:

By straining and rinsing the canned potatoes and green beans in cool water, you can greatly reduce their sodium content.

This can be served with a warm sourdough bread and put over pasta, but tastes great on its own.

VEGETABLE CHILI

1   onion, finely chopped

1   teaspoon crushed garlic

2   15-ounce cans whole tomatoes, finely diced

3   cups fresh mushrooms, finely chopped

2   green peppers, finely chopped

2   carrots, grated

2   zucchinis, finely chopped

1/8   teaspoon black pepper

1   teaspoon dried oregano, crushed

3   teaspoons chili powder

2   tablespoons flour

1   16-ounce can kidney beans, drained

1   shake of McCormick Hot Shot ™ (optional)

In large skillet, add 2 cups water, and simmer onion and garlic until tender.

Add all the vegetables and seasonings except the flour and beans.

Cover and simmer until all vegetables are tender, about 15 minutes.

In a separate small bowl, combine flour with 3 tablespoons of water, mixing slowly.

Add flour mixture very slowly to the chili, stirring constantly.

Add drained beans and cook, stirring often, until thickened (5~7 minutes).

Let simmer 5 more minutes.

If necessary, salt may be added to taste.

Serve hot with fat-free saltine crackers.

SERVES: 6
CALORIES: 119

I taste tested this on my good friend John Kuehl, who grew up eating real Texas Chili. I made him close his eyes and taste, and he was sure it was loaded with meat and greese. That was enough proof for me. When all these vegetables are simmered in the water and chili powder, it looks just like ground beef. This dish is an excellent source of both complex carbohydrates and protein.

WONTON MANDARIN SESAME CHICKEN

20	*wonton wrappers*
1	*tablespoon sesame seeds*
2	*8-ounce boneless, skinless chicken breasts*
1	*cup fresh-cut green beans*
1/2	*cup fat-free mayonnaise*
1	*bunch fresh chopped cilantro*
2	*teaspoons honey*
1	*teaspoon reduced-sodium soy sauce*
1	*small can mandarin oranges, drained*
	Dash black pepper
	Vegetable cooking spray

Pre-heat oven to 350 degrees.

Spray a muffin pan with the cooking spray, and line each space with a wonton skin, pressing the skin up against the inside of each well.

Bake for 8-10 minutes or until golden.

Remove from the oven and let cool.

Place the sesame seeds in a shallow baking dish, and bake for 5-7 minutes or until lightly toasted, stirring occasionally.

Remove and set aside to cool.

Bring two cups water to a boil.

Boil the chicken breasts until they turn white (about 10 minutes).

Add the green beans and simmer both 7 minutes more.

Drain.

Finely chop the chicken and add it to the bowl.

Add all of the remaining ingredients except the cilantro.

Mix well and spoon a tablespoon of the chicken mixture into each wonton cup.

Garnish with cilantro.

SERVES: 10
CALORIES: 120

. . . SIDE DISHES . . .

APRICOT STUFFING

1   celery stalk, sliced (1 cup)

1   onion, chopped

1 1/2 cups turkey broth or reduced sodium chicken
      broth

16   slices whole wheat bread, cubed and dried,
or

1   cup stuffing

2   tablespoons dried parsley

1 1/2 teaspoons poultry seasoning

1/4   teaspoon salt

1   cup egg substitute

1   cup chopped dried or fresh apricots
      Vegetable cooking spray

Preheat oven to 375 degrees.

In a small saucepan, combine celery, onion, and turkey broth.

Cook over medium high heat, bringing to a boil.

Reduce heat to low.

Cover and simmer 5 minutes or until all vegetables are tender.

Combine celery, broth, bread crumbs, parsley, poultry seasoning, salt, egg substitute, and apricots in a large bowl.

Spoon into a lightly sprayed 2-quart casserole dish.

Cover and bake for 1/2 hour.

SERVES: 8
CALORIES: 100

This offers great beta caro-tene at your Thanksgiving feast! Choose firm apricots, and allow to ripen in the refrigerator. Apricots can be bought fresh or dried. Both carry a good dose of potas-sium.

BAKED FRENCH FRIED POTATOES

2	**large baking potatoes**
1	**cup egg substitute**
1/2	**teaspoon garlic powder**
1	**tablespoon fat-free Parmesan cheese**
	Vegetable cooking spray

Preheat oven to 375 degrees.

Wash the potatoes and slice into oval pieces.

Slice each oval into matchsticks.

Line a baking sheet with foil and spray with cooking spray.

Pour the egg substitute into a shallow dish and add the garlic powder and Parmesan cheese.

Dip the potato slices into the egg mixture, coating completely.

Line the cookie sheet with the potatoes and bake for 35~45 minutes, turning often to brown each side.

Sprinkle with salt and pepper.

Serve warm, with ketchup if desired.

SERVES:	4
CALORIES:	73

CHICKEN FRIED RICE

1 1/3 cups water

1 1/3 cups Minute™ rice

1   cup egg substitute

1/3   cup onion, chopped (1 small)

2   tablespoons low-sodium soy sauce

2   4 ounce skinless chicken breasts, cooked & cut up

or

8   small cooked and peeled shrimp

Vegetable spray

Bring 1 cup of water to a boil and cook rice according to package directions.

Remove from heat, cover and let stand 5 minutes.

Spray 10-inch skillet, sauté onion, and scramble the egg substitute.

Add the rice.

Stir over medium heat until rice and onion are lightly browned (about 5 minutes).

Combine 1/3 cup water and soy sauce and stir into rice.

Add shrimp or chicken.

SERVES: 4

CALORIES: 84

CARROTS AU GRATIN

1/2   cup corn flake crumbs

1/3   cup chopped onion

3   tablespoons flour

1/8   teaspoon pepper

1 1/2 cups skimmed milk

1   4 1/2-ounce package fat-free shredded
      cheddar cheese

4   cups carrots (approximately 1 1/2 pounds),
      cooked until tender, drained and sliced

1/2   cup egg substitute

1   tablespoon parsley flakes
      Vegetable cooking spray

Preheat oven to 350 degrees.

Combine corn flake crumbs and egg substitute
and set aside.

Spray a medium-sized skillet with the cooking
spray.

Add parsley flakes and onions and sauté 4~7
minutes until tender.

In a separate small pan, add milk, salt and pepper.

Cook over low heat.

Add the flour slowly, stirring constantly until
liquid is thick and bubbly.

Stir in carrots to the milk mixture, then add the
parsley flakes and onions.

Spray the bottom of a shallow 1 1/2-quart baking

dish.

Pour the entire mixture into the baking dish.

Sprinkle with the corn flake crumb mixture and top with cheese and extra corn flakes.

Bake for 20 minutes, until cheese is melted and corn flakes are golden brown.

SERVES:	8
CALORIES:	213

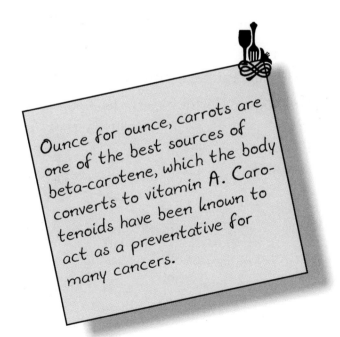

Ounce for ounce, carrots are one of the best sources of beta-carotene, which the body converts to vitamin A. Carotenoids have been known to act as a preventative for many cancers.

CREAMY MASHED POTATOES

8	medium baking potatoes
1	cup fat-free cream cheese, softened
1/4	cup light sour cream
1/2	cup fat-free Parmesan cheese
1/4	cup skim milk
	Dash of pepper

Preheat oven to 375 degrees.

Puncture tops of potatoes with fork and bake until tender (approx. 40 minutes).

Let cool and slice in half.

Scoop out inside of potatoes and put into a bowl.

Add the sour cream, cream cheese, skim milk, pepper, and Parmesan cheese.

Blend with an electric mixer or food processor.

SERVES: 8
CALORIES: 120

A terrific source of potassium, a mineral that modern diets so frequently lack. This recipe tastes butter-rich, yet is still pretty low in fat and calories.

FRESH ASPARAGUS WITH LEMON

1   *pound fresh asparagus*
     Juice of 1/2 lemon

Wash asparagus; snap stalks.

Place on vegetable steamer rack over boiling water; cover and steam for 5~6 minutes, just until barely tender.

To microwave:

Arrange asparagus in a single layer, tender tips toward center, in a microwave-proof baking dish.

Cover with plastic wrap (puncture wrap with a fork to allow steam to escape).

Cook 3~4 minutes, just until tender.

Drizzle with lemon juice.

SERVES: 12
CALORIES: 16

FRESH ASPARAGUS AND TOMATOES

2	*pounds fresh asparagus*
6	*medium tomatoes, thinly sliced*
1/2	*cup fat-free Parmesan cheese*
2	*tablespoons basil*
1/4	*teaspoon dill*
4	*tablespoons balsamic vinegar*

Cut off tough ends of asparagus.

Cook covered in 1/2 cup of boiling water for 4~6 minutes, or until crisp and tender.

Drain.

Place asparagus in ice water to stop the cooking process.

Drain and set aside.

Arrange slices of tomatoes around the edge of a platter.

Sprinkle with Parmesan cheese and drizzle with vinegar.

Arrange asparagus in center of platter.

Garnish with basil and dill.

SERVES: 4
CALORIES: 43

HERB ROASTED POTATOES

1   *cup fat-free Miracle Whip™*

1   *tablespoon garlic powder*

1   *tablespoon oregano*

1   *tablespoon onion powder*

2   *tablespoons water*

2   *pounds small red potatoes, quartered*

        Vegetable cooking spray

Preheat oven to 400 degrees.

Mix dressing, seasonings, and water in a large bowl.

Toss potatoes in the mixture, coating completely.

Spray a cookie sheet with vegetable cooking spray.

Place potatoes on the cookie sheet and bake for 30~40 minutes, until golden brown, turning after 15 minutes.

SERVES: 8

CALORIES: 116

The herbs and spices bring out the zing in these potatoes without loading up on the sodium. And garlic is getting high marks for healthy living.

MAPLE STUFFED SWEET POTATOES

4	*large sweet potatoes*
6	*tablespoons plain nonfat yogurt*
2	*tablespoons light maple syrup*
2	*tablespoons orange juice*
1	*tablespoon Dijon mustard*
1/4	*teaspoon cinnamon*
1/8	*teaspoon nutmeg*

Preheat oven to 375 degrees.

Wash sweet potatoes thoroughly, poke two holes in each and place in oven on rack.

Bake for 60 minutes.

Remove from oven and cool slightly.

Slice potatoes in half lengthwise and scoop out pulp, leaving shells.

Place shells on baking pan.

Using food processor or blender, blend pulp and remaining ingredients until smooth.

Spoon mixture evenly into shells.

Return to oven and bake for 10 minutes, or until golden brown.

SERVES: 8
CALORIES: 120

Believe it or not, when Columbus brought back the news about the new world, he also brought back the North American sweet potato. That information just might win you some $$$ some day in a trivia contest! Store in a cool dry place, but not in the refrigerator.

MEXICAN COUSCOUS

1   cup couscous

1/2   cup fat-free sour cream

1   15-ounce can pinto beans, rinsed and drained

1   4 1/2-ounce can chopped green chilies

1   tablespoon chopped dill

1 1/2 teaspoon ground cumin

1   cup (4 ounces) shredded fat-free cheddar cheese

       Vegetable cooking spray

Preheat oven to 350 degrees.

Prepare the couscous according to package directions.

In a large bowl, combine all ingredients except the cheese.

Spray the casserole dish with the cooking spray.

Combine the couscous with the other ingredients and pour into the casserole dish.

Bake for 20~25 minutes, or until heated through.

Remove from oven, sprinkle with the cheese, and bake for 5~7 more minutes.

SERVES: 4~6
CALORIES: 90

MICROWAVE BAKED APPLES

4   large apples
2   teaspoons sugar
1/2   teaspoon cinnamon

Remove core from the apples.

Cut apples into slices.

Cover the bottom of a glass baking dish with a thin layer of water.

Place apple slices in baking dish.

Add sugar and cinnamon.

Cover with wax paper.

Cook at full power for 3 minutes, or until apples are tender.

Growing up on these always left a great aroma throughout my home. So instead of paying $22.00 for a candle scented with this smell, bake your apples in the conventional oven at 350 degrees for one hour, and you too can have a home smelling of fresh, fall-orchard picked apples, even in Texas at 82 degrees.

SERVES: 8
CALORIES: 39

PASTA STUFFED TOMATOES

4	*ounces small pasta shells or spirals, uncooked*
4	*large tomatoes*
3	*tablespoons nonfat Miracle Whip™*
1	*tablespoon skim milk*
1	*teaspoon crushed garlic*
1/4	*teaspoon ground black pepper*
1	*cup fat-free grated Parmesan cheese*
1	*14 1/2-ounce can diced tomatoes*
	Dash of dill

Preheat oven to 350 degrees.

Cook pasta according to package, omitting salt.

Drain and rinse well.

Cut off tops of tomatoes and scoop out insides.

Turn upside down and drain on a paper towel for five minutes.

In a blender or food processor, blend dill, garlic, Miracle Whip, chopped tomatoes, milk, and pepper until smooth.

Add to pasta mixture.

Put tomatoes right side up in an 8-inch baking dish.

Add the mixture to each tomato.

Sprinkle with cheese.

Bake 20~30 minutes, until heated throughout.

SERVES: 4
CALORIES: 120

POTATO CHIPS

4   *medium-sized baking potatoes*

4   *cups ice cold water*

    Dash of garlic salt

    Vegetable cooking spray

Preheat oven to 450 degrees.

Wash the potatoes and slice very thin.

Put the slices in ice water and refrigerate for about 30 minutes (the water will prevent the potatoes from turning brown).

Drain potatoes and dry completely with paper towels.

Spray a cookie sheet with the cooking spray.

Spread enough of the chips on a baking sheet to cover the bottom without overlapping, and sprinkle with garlic salt.

Bake for 10 minutes, until brown on one side.

Turn over with tongs and bake for 5 minutes more.

Take out and let cool on a plate.

Repeat until all of the chips have been baked.

SERVES: **4~5**

CALORIES: **60**

ROASTED ASPARAGUS AND MUSHROOMS

1	*pound fresh asparagus, trimmed*
1	*pound Shiitake mushrooms, cleaned and trimmed*
1	*tablespoon olive oil*
1	*tablespoon fresh or dried rosemary, crushed*
	Dash of black pepper
	Dash of garlic powder

Preheat oven to 500 degrees.

Pour oil into a large plastic bag with a zip-lock seal.

Add asparagus and shake until the vegetable is coated with oil.

Add the rosemary and mushrooms and continue to gently shake until asparagus and mushrooms are covered.

Arrange the asparagus and mushrooms on a single layer on a baking sheet.

Season with pepper and garlic powder.

Bake for 10 minutes, until vegetables are crisp and tender.

SERVES: 4
CALORIES: 43

ROASTED NEW POTATOES

1   *dozen small white potatoes*

or

1   *15-ounce can whole white potatoes*
     Garlic salt
     Fresh rosemary
     Fresh thyme or dill
     Vegetable cooking spray

Preheat oven to 350 degrees.

Spray the bottom of a shallow baking pan with vegetable cooking spray.

Wash and peel fresh potatoes or rinse canned potatoes.

Place potatoes in bottom of baking pan.

Sprinkle with rosemary, garlic salt, and thyme.

Bake for 45 minutes, or until golden brown.

SERVES: 4~6
CALORIES: 60

TWICE-BAKED POTATOES

4	*large baking potatoes*
1	*8-ounce package fat-free cream cheese, softened*
1/3	*cup skimmed milk*
1/4	*teaspoon salt*
1/4	*cup chopped green onions*
	Dash of pepper
	Paprika

Heat oven to 350 degrees.

Wash potatoes very well.

Bake for 1 1/2 hours.

Cut potatoes in half lengthwise and scoop out centers, leaving 1/4 inch shell.

Pour centers into a mixing bowl and mash, adding softened cream cheese.

Stir well.

Add milk and seasonings.

Beat (either by hand or using a mixer) until soft and fluffy.

Add onions and spoon mixture back into shells.

Place filled shells on cookie sheet.

Sprinkle with paprika.

Bake for 20-25 minutes.

SERVES:	8
CALORIES:	120

Recipes For The Heart, Morsels For The Soul

VEGETABLE COUSCOUS

1/2   *cup yellow bell pepper, chopped*

1/2   *cup zucchini, sliced (1 small)*

1/4   *cup chopped onion*

3/4   *cup tomatoes, sliced and chopped (1 tomato)*

3/4   *cup fresh mushrooms, chopped*

1   *garlic clove, minced*

1 1/2   *cups chicken or vegetable broth*

1/4   *cup nonfat dairy creamer*

1   *cup couscous*

1/4   *cup chopped fresh parsley*

1/4   *teaspoon dried basil*

1/8   *teaspoon pepper*

        Vegetable cooking spray

Spray a 10-inch skillet and sauté peppers, zucchini, onions, and garlic until tender.

Add chicken broth and dairy creamer.

Bring to a boil and remove from heat.

Add couscous, parsley, basil, and pepper.

Cover and let set for 5 minutes, or until all liquid is absorbed.

Stir in chopped tomatoes.

Serve warm.

SERVES: 4
CALORIES: 110

. . . JEWISH COOKING . . .

KEEP YOUR HEART BEATING WITH HEALTHY JEWISH EATING

My love for Jewish cooking is the natural result of having grown up in Skokie, Illinois, with traditional Jewish parents. Holidays are a major part of Jewish tradition, and, of course, one can't properly observe a Jewish holiday without experiencing the rich flavors and smells of the food that accompanies each holiday.

And what would Jewish cooking be without a Jewish mother lovingly laboring in the kitchen? My own mother, Sabina Kamen-Handel, could always be found in our small kitchen, cooking up the most delicious brisket and sundry accompaniments: homemade chicken soup, challah bread, fruit compote potatoes and kishke.

Having been raised on these Friday Sabbath delicacies, is it any wonder that I longed to smell and re-experience them as an adult? For years, I struggled to maintain these traditions in my own home. Against the backdrop of a frantic 90s' lifestyle, however, this was very difficult. I often felt inadequate compared to my mother (who, by the way, can still be found in her home today in Houston, Texas, using some of her original cookware she was using when I was growing up).

Yet another blow to tradition came when I began my quest for a healthier lifestyle for my family. Traditional Jewish cooking is incredibly flavorful but, alas, high in fat. Combined with the "must-clear-your-plate" rule enforced by most Jewish mothers, this type of eating is about as far removed from heart-healthy as a person can get. What's a mother to do?

The turning point came in the spring of 1994, when my girlfriend, Wendy Geisler of Wendy's Kitchen, and I were approached to develop a new class about heart-healthy cooking for the Jewish holiday of Passover. After a long think-tank session, we developed a forum for incorporating Jewish traditions with healthy living. We began teaching a series of courses, "Cooking Without Kvetching" (Cooking Without Complaining). We launched the series with a course on low-fat Passover cooking called, "How To Pass Over The Fat, or, Schmooze about Schmaltz" (Talk about Fat). Wendy and I soon became known in the Jewish community of Arlington, Texas as The Lean Cuisine Team. Since then, I have done a great deal of consulting and developing of heart-healthy Jewish recipes.

In this section I have included some favorites inspired by years of eating holiday Jewish foods, and, of course, by my fond childhood memories of celebration feasts. I hope you find these recipes enriching and tasty as you incorporate them into your life.

LaChaim ... To Life!

During the Middle Ages, the Jewish people split into two main groups known as the Sephardic and the Ashkenazi. As a result, two very distinct culinary traditions have emerged over the centuries, and both have played a major role in the Passover Seder. While similar religious practices have remained consistent in both groups, their foods - due partly to climate and availability - have varied. Most Sephardim lived in the warm Mediterranean regions of Spain, Greece, Turkey, and North Africa, where fruits and vegetables were available year round. Ashkenazim, on the other hand, lived in the cooler climates of northeastern Europe, and their diet contained more grains, root vegetables and animal products.

This section contains low-fat Passover classics from both the Sephardic and Ashkenazim traditions. Whether or not you celebrate Passover, it is my hope that these recipes will help inspire you to embrace healthy eating...for life.

A NOTE ON INGREDIENTS...

Many of these recipes get their flavors from the culture of the Middle East. Here is a list of helpful ingredients, found in many grocery sores in the ethnic section.

Hummus: a spread made from chickpeas, spices and tahini.

Tahini: sesame seed butter, made from ground hulled sesame seeds.

Tabouli: a salad made from bulgur, fresh herbs and ground vegetables.

Pita Bread: a flat bread made from white or whole wheat flour.

Matzo: a flat bread made without leavening, usually eaten at the holiday of Passover.

CARROT TSIMMES

1   *pound carrots*

1   *8-ounce can crushed pineapples*

6   *ounces pitted prunes*

1/2   *cup water*

1/2   *cup orange juice*

1/2   *teaspoon ground ginger*

1/2   *teaspoon ground cinnamon*

1/4   *teaspoon salt*

Peel carrots.

Cook in boiling water for 20 minutes (or until soft & tender).

Drain & slice.

Combine crushed pineapple (with juice) and all remaining ingredients.

Simmer, covered, for 15 minutes over medium-low heat.

Serve warm.

SERVES: 4

CALORIES: 90

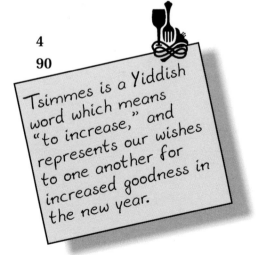

Tsimmes is a Yiddish word which means "to increase," and represents our wishes to one another for increased goodness in the new year.

EGGPLANT HUMMUS DIP

1	*large eggplant*
4	*cups cooked, drained chickpeas*
1	*teaspoon crushed garlic or 4 fresh garlic cloves*
1/2	*teaspoon ground coriander*
1/8	*teaspoon ground cayenne pepper*
1/2	*teaspoon black pepper*
1/2	*cup minced parsley*
	Dash of lemon juice

Preheat oven to 375 degrees.

Stab the eggplant with a fork and bake on a cookie sheet for 45 minutes.

Remove from the oven and cool.

Peel the skin off the eggplant and combine the eggplant and the remaining ingredients into the food processor.

Blend well until dip is smooth and creamy.

Chill and serve with pita bread or table crackers.

SERVES: 4~6

CALORIES: 18

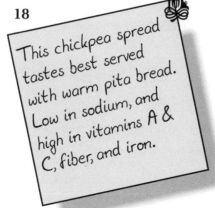

This chickpea spread tastes best served with warm pita bread. Low in sodium, and high in vitamins A & C, fiber, and iron.

EGGPLANT MATZO LASAGNA

3   cups sliced mushrooms

1   teaspoon crushed garlic

1/4   cup chopped fresh parsley

1/4   cup dry red wine (optional)

1   teaspoon dried basil

1   teaspoon dried oregano

1/4   teaspoon crushed red pepper

1/4   teaspoon black pepper

1   28-ounce can tomato pureé

1   large eggplant, peeled and cut into 1/2- inch
      slices (about 11/4 pounds)
      Vegetable cooking spray

1   15-ounce container nonfat ricotta cheese
      Nonfat Parmesan cheese, grated

3~5   slices of matzo

Preheat oven to 400 degrees.

Spray a skillet with the cooking spray.

Add mushrooms and garlic and sauté over a
medium heat for 5 minutes.

Stir in parsley, wine, basil, oregano, peppers and
tomato puree.

Cover the pan, lower the heat and simmer 30
minutes.

Bake the eggplant on a cookie sheet for 60 minutes.

Remove the eggplant from the baking sheet, and
let cool.

Lower oven temp to 350 degrees.

Slice the eggplant into slices and set aside.

Combine 1/4 cup Parmesan cheese and the ricotta cheese; stir well and set aside.

Spread 1/2 cup tomato mixture on the bottom of an 11x7-inch baking dish coated with cooking spray.

Arrange 1 1/2 slices of the matzo over the tomato mixture, and top the matzo with half of the ricotta cheese mixture, half of the eggplant, and half of the tomato mixture.

Repeat the layers, ending with the tomato mixture.

Sprinkle with the remaining Parmesan cheese.

Cover and bake (at 350 degrees) for 45 minutes.

Uncover and bake an additional 15 minutes.

Let stand and cool 5 minutes before serving.

SERVES: 6
CALORIES: 110

FRUIT LOKSHEN KUGEL

1   12-ounce package yolk-free noodles
3   ripe bananas, peeled and mashed
2   apples, cored, peeled and chopped
2   peaches, peeled and sliced
1/2 cup white raisins
1   teaspoon cinnamon
4   quarts water
     Vegetable cooking spray

Pre-heat oven to 350 degrees.

Bring water to a boil, add noodles and cook according to package.

Drain and rinse well.

Mix noodles with mashed bananas and cinnamon.

Lightly spray a 9 X 9 X 2 glass baking dish.

Layer noodle mixture with fruit and raisins on top.

Repeat process two more times.

Top with cinnamon.

Bake 40 minutes. Serve warm and enjoy!

SERVES: 6~8
CALORIES: 52

Lokshen kugel means "noodle pudding" in Yiddish. Kugels originated in Eastern Europe, and are usually made with potatoes or noodles. This is a great low-fat recipe for a summer luncheon menu.

MATZO VEGETABLE LASAGNA

1	cup tomato juice
1/2	teaspoon minced onion
1/2	teaspoon crushed garlic
1/2	teaspoon Italian seasonings
1	cup sliced onions
1/2	cup fresh mushrooms
4	sheets matzos (moistened until soggy)
1	6-ounce container low-fat cottage cheese
1	12-ounce package grated fat-free mozzarella cheese
	Dash of pepper
	Vegetable non-stick cooking spray

Preheat oven to 350 degrees.

Spray a skillet with the cooking spray.

Slice the onions and mushrooms and sauté 5~7 minutes over medium heat.

In a separate bowl, combine the tomato juice with the seasonings and mix well.

In a 8 inch square pan, layer the following:

>1/3 of the tomato juice mixture
>1 matzo
>1/3 of the sautéed veggies
>1/3 of the cottage cheese

Repeat two more layers.

Top with the grated cheese.

Bake for 25~30 minutes or until cheese is melted.

SERVES: 4~6
CALORIES: 75

This mouth-watering variation on a classic Italian dish is sure to satisfy even the most discriminating eaters. They won't believe it's low in fat and calories!

MEDITERRANEAN-STYLE VEGETABLE STEW

1	medium onion, chopped to equal 1 cup
1	medium bell pepper, cut into slices to equal 2 cups
2	small zucchini, cubed to equal 2 cups
1	small eggplant, cubed to equal 2 cups
1	tablespoon crushed garlic
2	medium tomatoes, cut into chunks to equal 2 cups
1	cup tomato juice
2	tablespoons tomato paste
3	tablespoons dry red wine
1	bay leaf
1	teaspoon basil and marjoram
1/2	teaspoon oregano
	Dash of ground rosemary
	Dash of black pepper
	Fresh parsley, chopped
	Vegetable cooking spray

Spray the bottom of a large cooking pot with cooking spray.

Add the garlic, bay leaf and onion.

Sauté over a medium heat until the onion becomes tender and begins to turn transparent.

Add the eggplant, wine and tomato juice.

Mix well and add the herbs.

Stir and cover to simmer 10~15 minutes over a low heat.

Add the zucchini and peppers, cover, and simmer another 10 minutes.

Add pepper, tomatoes, and tomato paste.

Mix well.

Continue to stew and simmer 20~30 minutes.

Just before serving, add fresh parsley.

SERVES:	4~6
CALORIES:	65

You may serve this on a bed of rice or couscous accompanied by a low-fat sourdough bread.

PASSOVER APPLE CRISP

5	medium Granny Smith Apples (about 1 1/2 pounds)
1/2	cup sugar
1	teaspoon ground cinnamon
2	teaspoons lemon juice
	Vegetable cooking spray
1/2	cup unsalted matzo meal
1/3	cup sugar
1/4	cup slivered almonds (optional)
1/8	teaspoon salt
	I Can't Believe It's Not Butter™ pump spray

Preheat oven to 350 degrees.

Peel, core and cut the apples into 1/4 inch slices.

Combine apple slices, sugar, cinnamon and lemon juice in a separate bowl.

Toss lightly.

Spray an 11 x 7- inch baking dish with the vegetable cooking spray.

Spoon the apple mixture into the baking dish and set aside.

Combine the matzo meal, sugar, almonds, and salt, mixing well.

Sprinkle over the apple mixture.

Using the pump spray, lightly coat the top of the mixture.

Bake for one hour or until browned.

This tasty dish, a wonderful combination of traditional ethnic foods and healthful, sweet flavors, is proof that you don't have to abandon good health during a festive holiday meal.

PASSOVER APPLESAUCE NOODLE KUGEL

1	12-ounce package Passover noodles
1	5-ounce jar unsweetened applesauce
1/2	cup white raisins
1	teaspoon cinnamon
1/4	cup sugar
1/2	cup egg substitute
	Vegetable cooking spray

Preheat oven to 350 degrees.

Cook the noodles according to the package directions.

Drain and rinse.

Combine with all other ingredients.

Spray the bottom of a 1 1/2 quart casserole dish.

Spread mixed ingredients into the pan.

Bake for 60 minutes.

SERVES: 6
CALORIES: 18

RUSSIAN CHAROSET

1   *pound pears (2~3 medium pears or a 12 ounce can) peeled, cored, drained, and grated*

1   *pound apricots (7~8 fresh or 1½ cups dried and chopped)*

1   *small can mandarin oranges (drained and sliced)*

2   *tablespoons slivered almonds*

Toss all the ingredients together in a bowl.

Chill and stir before serving.

SERVES: 8

CALORIES: 72

PASSOVER VEGETARIAN KISHKE

1/2   *cups mushrooms, chopped*

4   *stalks celery, chopped*

2   *carrots, grated*

2   *onions, peeled and minced*

2   *cups water*

1   *tablespoon olive oil*

2 1/2 *cups matzo meal*

1   *tablespoon paprika*

2   *teaspoons garlic powder*

1/4   *teaspoon pepper*

1   *teaspoon salt*

Pre-heat oven to 350 degrees.

Mix all the ingredients together in a large bowl.

Spoon 1/4 of mixture onto a large piece of aluminum foil that has been sprayed with a small but even coat of vegetable spray.

Roll mixture into an 8-inch long cylinder.

Seal both ends of foil.

Repeat to form 4 cylinders.

Place cylinders on cookie sheet.

Bake for 45 minutes.

Turn cylinders over, and bake an additional 30~45 minutes longer.

Remove foil and serve sliced and warm.

SERVES: 4~6
CALORIES: 220

SPINACH MATZO BAKE

1	package frozen spinach, thawed and drained
1	onion, finely chopped
3	matzo squares, softened in warm water
3/4	cup egg substitute
1	tablespoon skim milk
1	package fat-free grated cheddar cheese
	Dash of pepper
1/2	cup chopped fresh dill
	Vegetable cooking spray

Preheat oven to 375 degrees.

Spray the skillet and sauté the chopped onions for 4~7 minutes.

Add the spinach and sauté for 3 additional minutes.

Pour egg substitute into a shallow dish, add skim milk and dip one matzo sheet into the mixture.

Spray a square casserole dish and line the bottom of the dish with the matzo sheet.

Spread half of the spinach-onion mixture on top of the matzo and cover with 1/3 of the cheese.

Continue to layer, making the cheese the top layer.

Sprinkle with pepper and fresh dill.

Bake for 40~45 minutes until top is golden.

Serve warm.

SERVES: 4
CALORIES: 116

SWEET ISRAELI CHICKEN

3   pounds skinless, boneless chicken breasts

24   dried apricots, cut up

4   ounces apricot marmalade

1/2   cup raisins

1/2   cup grape juice

1 1/2 tablespoons vinegar

1   tablespoon crushed garlic

1   large onion, sliced thin

1/2   cup honey

Preheat oven to 350 degrees.

Rinse chicken and lay into a glass baking dish.

Combine remaining ingredients in a separate bowl, mixing well.

Pour the mixture evenly over the chicken, making sure to cover all breasts well.

Bake, covered, for 1 hour.

Remove foil and bake an additional 1/2 hour, or until golden brown.

I have been eating this dish since my mother-in-law, Vivian Pock, used to serve it to me and my husband Les when we were just newlyweds. That was many years ago, and the recipe — like the memories it inspires — just gets better with time.

SERVES: 4

CALORIES: 221

. . . DESSERTS . . .

APPLE PANDOWDY

1	can of sliced apples or apple pie filling

or

2~3	cups of cooked, softened apples
1 1/2	cups flour
1	cup sugar
1 1/2	teaspoon baking powder
2	egg whites, beaten with a fork or whisk
2	teaspoons cinnamon
	Cinnamon sugar
	Pinch of salt
	Vegetable cooking spray

Preheat oven to 350 degrees.

Lightly spray a glass 9x 9-inch baking dish with the cooking spray.

Cover the bottom of the pan with the sliced apples.

Mix together the flour and the sugar.

To this mixture, add baking powder, salt, egg whites, and cinnamon.

Using a fork, blend the dough until it starts to form a ball.

Lightly flour a rolling pin and roll the dough out into a 9x9-inch top crust.

Spread the crust over the apples.

Spray the top of the crust with the cooking spray and sprinkle cinnamon sugar on top.

Bake 30~40 minutes, or until the top has browned.

SERVES: 5
CALORIES: 101

This dish can be served either warm or cool. You may want to top this cobbler with fat-free yogurt.

APPLE CRANBERRY PANDOWDY

1   *20-ounce can sliced apples or apple pie filling*

1   *16-ounce can whole berry cranberry sauce*

3/4 *cup sugar*

2   *teaspoons cinnamon*

1/4 *cup flour*

2   *tablespoons light brown sugar*

1 1/2 *teaspoons oil substitute (apple sauce or*
      Lighter Bake™)

3/4 *cup Cracklin Oat Bran™ cereal*
      Vegetable cooking spray

Preheat oven to 375 degrees.

Lightly spray a 9x13-inch baking dish with vegetable cooking spray.

In a large bowl, combine the apples, cranberry sauce, sugar, 1 teaspoon cinnamon, and 1 tablespoon flour.

Mix well.

Pour the mixture into the baking dish.

Pour the Cracklin Oat Bran™ into a plastic bag, seal and pound to crunch it down.

Pour the Cracklin Oat Bran™, the remaining flour and brown sugar into a bowl, and mix well.

Add in the oil substitute and mix.

Pour the topping over the apple mixture and bake 40~50 minutes.

Let cool.

SERVES: 8
CALORIES: 90

This is a great warm side dish. Remember, you can always make this with left-over cranberry sauce from Thanksgiving. This can be made ahead of time, frozen, and served at the winter holidays. Loaded with flavonoids that act as antioxidants, to fight off many illnesses. You can cut down on some of your added sugar, as cranberries can be cooked down, softened and sweetened with brown sugar or cinnamon sugar, which will also make the house smell great.

BAKED BANANAS

1 1/2 teaspoons lemon juice
2   teaspoons lemon rind
1   tablespoon brown sugar
4   bananas, sliced and peeled

Preheat oven to 375 degrees.

Brush mixture over bananas.

Bake for 15 minutes.

SERVES: 4
CALORIES: 24

BANANA BREAD

5	*ripe bananas*
1/2	*cup egg substitute*
1/4	*cup unsweetened applesauce*
2	*cups flour*
3/4	*cup sugar*
1	*teaspoon salt*
1	*teaspoon baking powder*
1	*small carrot, grated*
1/2	*cup raisins*
	Vegetable cooking spray

Preheat oven to 350 degrees.

In large mixing bowl, mash bananas with a wooden spoon.

Add eggs, flour, sugar, salt, baking powder, carrot, and raisins.

Stir well.

Spray a 9x5-inch loaf pan with vegetable cooking spray.

Pour in the batter and bake for 1 hour.

Cut into 8 slices.

SERVES:	8
CALORIES:	130

COCOA TRUFFLES

1/2   *cup dried apricots, chopped*

1/2   *cup pitted prunes, chopped*

1/2   *cup white golden raisins (3 ounces)*

1   *tablespoon honey*

1   *tablespoon cocoa (sweetened)*

2   *cups sifted powdered sugar*

Add all of the ingredients except the cocoa to a blender or food processor.

Blend until the mixture becomes sticky (you may have to stop often because the mixture may become too dry).

Shape the mixture into small bite-sized balls.

Wrap in waxed paper and refrigerate for 1 hour.

Roll the balls in the cocoa.

Sprinkle with powdered sugar.

Store tightly covered.

SERVES: 10
CALORIES: 82

CHOCOLATE DEVIL'S FOOD CAKE

1/2   cup prune baby food

3/4   cup water

1/4   cup egg substitute

1 1/2 teaspoons vanilla

1   cup unsweetened cocoa powder

1 1/2 teaspoons baking powder

1/4   teaspoon baking soda

1   cup + 1 tablespoon sugar

1   cup + 1 tablespoon flour

1   container fat-free non-dairy whipped topping

*   Vegetable cooking spray*

Preheat oven to 350 degrees.

Spray a 9-inch square baking dish with the cooking spray and set aside.

In a mixing bowl, combine water, prune baby food, egg substitute and vanilla.

Blend in a food processor or blender, until ingredients are mixed thoroughly.

Add remaining ingredients to the cake mixture.

Pour batter into the cake pan and bake 30 minutes, or until a toothpick comes out clean when inserted into the middle of the cake.

Cool.

When the cake is cooled, add a thin layer of the whipped topping.

Cut into squares and serve.

Can be topped with fresh fruit.

SERVES:	12
CALORIES:	136

LIGHTER CHOCOLATE CHIP COOKIES

1	*cup packed brown sugar*
1/2	*cup sugar*
1/2	*cup Lighter Bake™ or oil substitute*
1/4	*cup egg substitute*
1	*teaspoon vanilla*
2 1/4 cups all-purpose flour	
1	*teaspoon baking powder*
1/2	*teaspoon baking soda*
1/2	*teaspoon salt*
1	*12-ounce package reduced fat semi-sweet chocolate flavor baking chips*
	Vegetable cooking spray

Preheat oven to 375 degrees.

Coat a cookie sheet with vegetable cooking spray and set aside.

In a mixing bowl, combine egg substitute, brown sugar, white sugar and Lighter Bake.

Add to food processor for a short time.

Stir well.

In a separate bowl combine flour, baking powder, baking soda and salt.

Combine this mixture to the liquid mixture.

Stir well and add chocolate chips.

Blend well.

Drop a small rounded spoonful onto the prepared baking sheet.

Bake for 10~15 minutes.

Remove from the oven and let cool on cooling racks.

SERVES:	**42**
CALORIES:	**100**

DESSERTS

LEMON CHEESECAKE

2   cups low-fat graham cracker crumbs, crushed

3   8-ounce bars fat free cream cheese, softened

2   14-ounce cans Eagle Brand™ Fat-Free
       Sweetened Condensed Milk

1/4   cup egg substitute

1/2   cup lemon juice

1   teaspoon vanilla extract

1/2   cup unsifted flour

1   cup fresh assorted fruit

3   tablespoons nonfat liquid butter substitute
       Vegetable cooking spray

Preheat oven to 300 degrees.

Spray the bottom of an 8 inch springform pan with cooking spray.

Sprinkle crumbs on the bottom of the pan.

Using a mixer, beat softened cream cheese and liquid butter until creamy.

Add in milk, beating until smooth.

Add egg substitute, lemon juice, and vanilla.

Mix well.

Slowly stir in flour.

Pour into prepared pan.

Bake for 50~55 minutes or until center is set.

Cool for 40 minutes.

Chill.

Serve topped with fruit.

Refrigerate leftovers.

SERVES: 10
CALORIES: 210

To crush the crumbs, put 8~10 graham crackers in a zip-lock plastic bag and crush them finely with a rolling pin.

MINI CHERRY CHEESECAKES

12   *reduced-fat vanilla wafers*

3   *8-ounce packages cream cheese (2 fat-free and 1 light)*

3/4 *cup sugar*

1   *teaspoon vanilla*

1/2 *cup egg substitute*

1   *8-ounce can cherry pie filling*
      Mini muffin papers

Preheat oven to 325 degrees.

Put one wafer flat side down in the bottom of the muffin paper.

Beat the cream cheese, sugar, and vanilla with an electric mixer or food processor until well blended.

Add egg substitute and beat until creamy.

Pour the cream cheese mixture over each wafer to fill each cup.

Bake for 30 minutes.

Cool before removing from the pan (you may refrigerate overnight).

Top with pie filling just before serving.

SERVES: 12
CALORIES: 140

PEACH COBBLER

1	*cup flour*
1	*cup sugar*
1	*teaspoon baking powder*
2	*egg whites*
1/4	*teaspoon cinnamon*
1/4	*teaspoon nutmeg*
2	*cans sliced peaches in light syrup*
	Vegetable cooking spray
	Pinch salt

Preheat oven to 350 degrees.

Lightly spray a 9x 9-inch glass baking dish with vegetable cooking spray.

Lay 3 cups of sliced peaches on the bottom.

In a medium bowl, mix the flour with the sugar, baking powder, salt, egg whites, cinnamon, and nutmeg.

Spread over the peaches, covering completely.

Bake 30 minutes.

SERVES: 6
CALORIES: 97

PUMPKIN RICOTTA CHEESECAKE

12   *low-fat graham crackers, crumbled*

1 1/3 cups *instant nonfat dry milk powder*

3/4   *cup non-fat ricotta cheese*

3/4   *cup egg substitute*

2/3   *cup low-fat (1%) cottage cheese*

1/2   *cup canned pumpkin*

1/4   *cup firmly-packed light brown sugar*

1   *tablespoon lemon juice*

1/2   *teaspoon cinnamon*

1/2   *teaspoon vanilla extract*

        Vegetable cooking spray

Preheat oven to 300 degrees.

Spray an 8-inch springform pan with nonstick cooking spray. Sprinkle bottom of pan with the graham cracker crumbs.

In a blender or food processor, blend the remaining ingredients until smooth. Pour mixture into prepared pan.

Bake 50~60 minutes.

Cool completely on rack.

Cover and refrigerate until ready to serve.

SERVES: 8

CALORIES: 160

RASPBERRY CHEESE PARFAIT

1   cup nonfat ricotta cheese
1   cup nonfat cream cheese, softened
1   bag frozen raspberries
1   tablespoon raspberry all-fruit spread
1   dash nonfat, non-dairy whipped topping
     Sprinkles

Blend the ricotta cheese and cream cheese together well.

Combine the frozen raspberries with the all-fruit spread.

In a clear parfait glass, alternate layers of the cheese mixture and the raspberries until you reach the top.

Top off with whipped topping and sprinkles.

SERVES: 4
CALORIES: 144

RICE PUDDING

2   cups instant rice
2 1/2 cups skim milk
1   teaspoon salt
1/4   teaspoon cinnamon
1/3   cup sugar
1/2   cup egg substitute
1/2   teaspoon vanilla
      Dash of nutmeg

Cook rice according to the package directions.

Combine rice, milk, sugar, salt, and cinnamon.

Pour into a saucepan and bring to a rolling boil, stirring constantly.

Reduce heat and cook uncovered for 15 minutes (keep at slow boil).

Slowly beat in the egg substitute.

Add vanilla and beat some more.

Sprinkle with nutmeg.

Refrigerate until thick (about 2 hours).

SERVES: **8~10**
CALORIES: **90**

STRAWBERRY ANGEL CAKE DELIGHT

1   10-inch angel food cake
1   pint crushed frozen strawberries, thawed
1   tablespoon skim milk
1   pint fresh strawberries, sliced
1   tub nonfat whipped topping, thawed
     Fresh mint leaves

Cut cake horizontally into 3 layers.

Place layer number one on a serving cake platter.

Blend crushed strawberries, milk and 1 1/2 cups whipped topping into a large bowl.

Spread 1/2 of the strawberry mixture on layer number one.

Arrange 1/2 of the sliced strawberries on top of the strawberry mixture.

Repeat for layer two.

Place the third layer of cake on the top.

Frost the top and sides with remaining whipped topping.

Refrigerate 1 hour or until ready to serve.

Decorate the top and sides with sliced strawberries and fresh mint.

SERVES: **10**
CALORIES: **41**

STRAWBERRY AND BANANA PUDDING PIE

15~20 honey graham crackers, crushed

2   medium bananas, sliced and dipped in lemon juice

1   cup fresh strawberries (10 medium), sliced

2   3-ounce bars cream cheese (1 lite, 1 fat-free), softened

7   ounces (1/2 can) lite Eagle Brand™ Sweetened Condensed Milk

1   4-ounce package instant vanilla pudding mix Skim milk (as called for on the pudding package)

1   cup fat-free whipped topping

Line pie plate with the crushed graham crackers.

Top with the mixed bananas and strawberries.

In a separate bowl, beat the cream cheese, slowly beating in half of the sweetened milk until creamy.

Heat mixture over low flame, beating constantly, until creamy.

Pour over the pie to make the next layer.

Mix the vanilla pudding with skim milk until creamy, according to the package directions.

Fold in the whipped topping.

Pour over the pie to make the top layer.

Serves: 8
Calories: 140

Top with sliced strawberries.

Chill and refrigerate.

STRAWBERRY ICE DESSERT

3   *egg whites*

1   *squirt of lemon juice*

2   *cups fresh strawberries, hulled and blended in the blender*

1/2   *cup sugar*

      Fat- free non-dairy whipped topping

Beat the egg whites until stiff peaks form.

To the eggs, add the lemon juice or fresh lemon.

Blend the clean, washed strawberries until smooth and fine.

Add the sugar slowly to the strawberry mixture and blend again.

Slowly add the beaten egg mixture to the strawberries and beat again for 8~12 minutes, stirring occasionally with a spatula (the mixture should fill a large bowl).

Transfer to a large, covered container and freeze.

This mixture will keep for 2~3 weeks in the freezer.

When served, top with the whipped topping.

SERVES: 6

CALORIES: 71

TIRAMISU

20   ladyfingers (cut in half) or cubed angle food
     cake
2   6-ounce packages light cream cheese
1   6-ounce package fat free cream cheese
1 1/2 cups sugar
1/4 cup skim milk
1   cup strong coffee or espresso, chilled
2   tablespoons dark rum or 1 tablespoon rum
     extract
1   tablespoon unsweetened cocoa powder
1   package fat-free vanilla pudding
     Grated semisweet chocolate or sprinkles
     (optional)

In a medium mixing bowl or food processor, mix the cream cheese mixture while slowly adding skim milk and sugar.

Cream until smooth. (It is best to soften the cream cheese at room temperature before creaming)

Break the ladyfingers into bite-sized pieces and arrange half on the bottom of the glass bowl.

Stir together the rum and coffee, and drizzle half of the mixture over the ladyfingers. (Ladyfingers are very spongy and absorb the liquid very quickly.)

Add the cream cheese mixture, followed by another layer of ladyfingers.

Mix the pudding according to the package directions, and add a layer of pudding.

Garnish with cocoa powder, sprinkles, or grated chocolate.

Cover and chill for 2~24 hours before serving.

SERVES: 15

CALORIES: 98

This is an Italian dessert that means, "PICK ME UP!" It's high in flavor, but this version is not that high in calories.

TRIFLE

1   *angel food cake*

1   *16-ounce container fat-free non-dairy whipped topping*

1   *4-ounce package vanilla or chocolate instant pudding*

1   *package frozen berries, thawed (strawberries, blueberries, cherries or peaches, or 1 cup fresh of each kind)*

1   *can pie filling (cherry, blueberry, peach, or your favorite)*

Cut the angel food cake into 1 inch cubes.

Layer the bottom of a clear trifle bowl or glass dish with approximately 20 cubes.

Add one layer of berries.

Add a layer of whipped topping.

Add one more layer of angel food cubes.

Prepare the instant pudding according to the package directions in a separate bowl, and add it to the next layer.

Add another layer of berries and top with the remaining whipped topping.

Garnish with sliced fresh strawberries or fresh blueberries.

Cover and chill in the refrigerator for 1 hour before serving.

SERVES: 10~15

CALORIES: 115

ZUCCHINI BREAD

2   cups sugar

1/2   cup egg substitute

1   cup applesauce

2 3/4 cups (2 large) unpeeled zucchini, grated

1   teaspoon cinnamon

3   teaspoons vanilla

2 1/4 cups flour

2   teaspoon baking soda

1/2   teaspoons baking powder

1   cup nuts (optional)
       Vegetable cooking spray

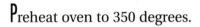

Preheat oven to 350 degrees.

Combine all of the dry ingredients.

Put the zucchini through the food processor.

Combine the zucchini mixture with the dry ingredients.

Add the egg substitute, applesauce, and vanilla, and beat for 5 minutes.

Spray a loaf pan with cooking spray and pour the batter into the pan.

Bake for 1 hour.

Check for doneness, and continue to cook for 15~20 minutes, or until a toothpick or knife, inserted in the center, comes out dry.

SERVES: 4
CALORIES: 144

TWO LAYER PUMPKIN PIE

1   4-ounce package nonfat cream cheese,
     softened
1   tablespoon non-fat French vanilla half and
     half or Coffee Mate™ Non-Dairy Creamer
1   tablespoon sugar
1 1/2 cups fat free non-dairy topping
1   reduced fat pre-formed graham cracker pie
     crust
1   16-ounce can pumpkin pie filling
1   4-ounce package French vanilla flavored
     instant pudding and pie filling
1   teaspoon ground cinnamon
1/2 teaspoon ground ginger
1/4 teaspoon ground cloves
1   cup skim milk

Mix softened cream cheese with 1 tablespoon half and half.

Add sugar and mix in a large bowl, using a wire whisk, until creamy.

Add whipped topping and mix gently.

Spread on the bottom of the pie crust.

In a separate bowl, pour skim milk, pumpkin, pudding mix, and spices.

Beat with whisk until thick and creamy.

Spread over the cream cheese layer.

Refrigerate for approximately four hours or until pie sets.

SERVES: 8
CALORIES: 127

Ginger can act like an aspirin, keeping the blood from clotting and helping to keep heart disease at bay! Pumpkin is a fruit, not a vegetable, since it is a member of the melon family. It's loaded with carotenes, fiber, and potassium, so eat year round! But remember, it's not calorie free, and many of those calories are coming from sugar.

. . . KIDS' COOKING . . .

BUGS ON A LOG

1   **bag of celery sticks**
1   **package lite cream cheese, softened**
1   **box raisins**

Cut celery sticks into 4-inch pieces.

Spread a layer of the softened cream cheese on top of the celery stick (log).

Top the cream cheese with a handful of raisins (bugs).

SERVES: 6
CALORIES: 18

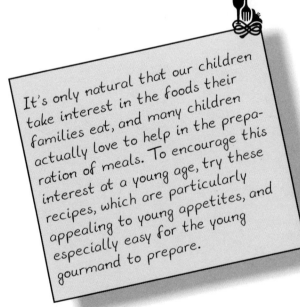

It's only natural that our children take interest in the foods their families eat, and many children actually love to help in the preparation of meals. To encourage this interest at a young age, try these recipes, which are particularly appealing to young appetites, and especially easy for the young gourmand to prepare.

BUNNY SALAD

1   *leaf lettuce*

1   *pear half*

1   *mini marshmallow*

2   *raisins*

1   *Red Hots ™ candy,*

or

1   *maraschino cherry*

For each bunny:

On a small plate, place one large lettuce leaf, forming a circle.

Place the pear half, flat side down, on top of the lettuce leaf.

Use two raisins as the bunny's eyes; put them on the small end of the pear.

Add the Red Hot or cherry as the bunny's nose.

Place the marshmallow at the opposite end of the pear to form the bunny's tail.

SERVES: 1
CALORIES: 75

CANDLE SALAD

1   *can pineapple rings*
4   *bananas*
1   *jar maraschino cherries*
1   *head leafy lettuce*

Place a pineapple ring on a small bed of leafy lettuce.

Place half or a whole peeled banana (depending on size) in the center of the pineapple ring (it should stand up by itself).

Cut off the pointed end of the banana.

Make a flame for your candle by placing a maraschino cherry on one end of a toothpick and poking the other end into the top of the banana.

SERVES: 4
CALORIES: 35

CINNAMON-APPLE QUESADIILLAS

2   *fat-free flour tortillas*
1/2   *cup chunky applesauce*
1   *teaspoon cinnamon sugar*
1   *tablespoon sifted powdered sugar*
        Fat-free vanilla yogurt
        Vegetable cooking spray

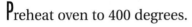

Preheat oven to 400 degrees.

Place one tortilla on a baking sheet sprayed with low-fat cooking spray.

Spread applesauce over tortilla.

Sprinkle cinnamon sugar over apple sauce.

Top with second tortilla, and spray lightly with cooking spray.

Sprinkle with cinnamon sugar and powdered sugar.

Bake for six to eight minutes, or until golden brown.

Cool for two minutes.

Cut into quarters and dip in vanilla yogurt (optional).

Eat & enjoy!

SERVES: 2
CALORIES: 97

DIRT CUPS

Instant chocolate pudding mix
Skim milk
Snack Wells™ lowfat chocolate sandwich
cookies
Gummi Worms™

Mix pudding with skim milk per package directions.

Crumble 10 cookies in a plastic sandwich bag.

In a clear glass bowl or new (clean) potting planter, layer pudding & cookies.

Add crumbled cookies for top layer.

Place Gummi Worms on top of "dirt" mixture.

SERVES:	10
CALORIES:	70

Yes, I know... this sounds "dirty!" But the kids just go wild over it, and it's so easy to make, they probably won't even ask for your help. Cleaning up afterward, however, is another matter!

FRUIT KABOBS WITH DIP

DIP

1	*cup vanilla fat-free yogurt*
2	*tablespoons orange juice*
1	*teaspoon grated orange rind*

On skewers, alternate chunks of pineapple, fresh strawberries, kiwi fruit, and bananas.

Combine dip ingredients.

Cover and chill for 2 hours.

Garnish with rind and serve.

SERVES:	**8**
CALORIES:	**15**

ICE CREAM CONE CUPCAKES

1	*box angel food cake mix*
12	*ice cream cones (flat-bottom safety cones)*
1	*6-ounce container nonfat, non-dairy whipped topping*
	Topping: sprinkles, Gummi Bears™ or Red-Hots™
	Vegetable cooking spray or muffin cups

Preheat oven per instructions on cake mix package.

Prepare the angel food cake according to package directions.

Pour the batter into the ice cream cones, filling each cone 3/4 of the way up.

Place one cone in each well of the cupcake pan.

Bake cones according to the angel food package instructions.

Remove from oven and let cool.

When cooled, add a scoop of cool whip to each cone and sprinkle with toppings.

SERVES: 12
CALORIES: 60

TURKEY HOT DOGS

1   *turkey hot dog*
1   *soft low-fat tortilla (either corn or flour)*
     Mustard (optional)

Cook the hot dog for 3~4 minutes in boiling water.
Cool.

Place the hot dog on a tortilla and spread with
mustard or cranberry sauce, if desired.

Roll the tortilla around the hot dog and secure
with a toothpick.

Wrap in foil.

SERVES: 1
CALORIES: 77

YOGURT POPSICLES

1   *cup plain, fat-free yogurt*
1   *banana, sliced*
1   *teaspoon vanilla*
1   *cup fruit juice or fruit chunks*
    (Our favorites: orange juice or peaches)

Blend ingredients together and pour into small paper cups.

Freeze.

When yogurt mixture is half frozen, place a plastic spoon or popsicle stick in each cup.

To serve, turn cup upside down and run hot water over it until the popsicle slips out.

Let children keep the cup as a holder.

SERVES: 4~5
CALORIES: 19

A nutritious alternative to the frozen treats you buy in the store, and the kids really love them.

APPENDICES

APPENDIX A:
HOW MUCH OF A GOOD THING?

O nce upon a time, all you had to know in order to plan a balanced diet was to include meat, fruits and vegetables, dairy products, and the "staff of life", bread. As science progressed, however, we became more able to accurately quantify the elements our bodies needed, and the U. S. Food and Drug Administration came up with a standard for Recommended Daily Allowances for different vitamins, minerals, and other nutrients.

...new initials... new values.... and a clear description of what they actually stand for.

Everything went along swimmingly until further research showed that these values were not comprehensive enough, and left too many gaps. In order to rectify the situation and fill in the blanks, the Food and Drug Administration (or FDA, as those initial-happy government folk like to call it) came up with some new initials to indicate the new values. Below, you will see a few of those collections of initials, along with a (hopefully) clear description of what they actually stand for.

- **RDAs (Recommended Dietary Allowances):** a set of estimated nutrient allowances established by the National Academy of Sciences. It is updated periodically to reflect current scientific knowledge. (However, see RDI below.)
- **RDIs (Reference Daily Intakes):** a set of dietary references based on the Recommended Dietary Allowances for essential vitamins and minerals and,

in selected groups, protein. The name "RDI" replaces the term "U.S. RDA."

- **DRVs (Daily Reference Values):** a set of dietary references that applies to fat, saturated fat, cholesterol, carbohydrate, protein, fiber, sodium, and potassium.
- **DVs (Daily Values):** a new dietary reference term that will appear on food labels. It is made up of two sets of references, DRVs and RDIs.

On the following pages, you will find FDA tables which detail the recommended values for the basic nutrients. Figure 1, below, lists the Daily Reference Values (DRV) for the major food components, based upon intake of 2,000 calories a day for adults and children over 4 only.

Food Component	DRV
Fat	65 grams (g)
Saturated fatty acids	20 g
Cholesterol	300 milligrams (mg)
Total carbohydrate	300 g
Fiber	25 g
Sodium	2,400 mg
Potassium	3,500 mg
Protein**	50 g

Figure 1

**DRV for protein does not apply to certain populations; Reference Daily Intake (RDI) for protein has been established for these groups, and appears in Figure 1a, on the next page.

Group	RDI
Children 1 to 4 years	16 g
Infants under 1 year	14 g
Pregnant women	60 g
Nursing mothers	65 g

Figure 1a

DRVs for the energy-producing nutrients (fat, carbohydrate, protein, and fiber) are based on the number of calories consumed per day. For labeling purposes, 2,000 calories has been established as the reference for calculating percent Daily Values. This level was chosen, in part, because many health experts say it approximates the maintenance calorie requirements of the group most often targeted for weight reduction: postmenopausal women.

Labels — at least on larger packages — will include a footnote on the nutrition panel in which daily values for selected nutrients for both a 2,000- and a 2,500-calorie diet are listed. Manufacturers have the option of listing daily values for other calorie levels, if label space allows and as long as the Daily Values for the other two levels are listed, too.

Whatever the calorie level, DRVs for the energy-producing nutrients are always calculated as follows:

- **Fat** is based on 30 percent of calories
- **Saturated fat** is based on 10 percent of calories
- **Carbohydrate** is based on 60 percent of calories
- **Protein** is based on 10 percent of calories. (Note the exceptions listed in Figure 1a.)
- **Fiber** is based on 11.5 g of fiber per 1,000 calories.

For example, someone who consumes 3,000 calories a day — a teenaged boy, for example — would have a recommended fat intake of 100 grams *or less* per day [30% of 3,000 = 900; 900 (calories) divided by 9 (calories per gram of fat) = 100 g]. Didn't know there was going to be math, did you?

The DRVs for cholesterol, sodium and potassium — which do not contribute calories — remain the same no matter what the level of calorie intake.

Because of the links between certain nutrients and diseases, DRVs for some nutrients represent the uppermost limit that is considered desirable. As we learned, the hard way, eating too much fat or cholesterol, for example, increases the risk of heart disease. Also, taking in too much sodium can heighten the risk of high blood pressure in some people.

For these reasons, food labels will show DVs for fats and sodium as follows:

- Total fat: less than 65 g
- Saturated fat: less than 20 g
- Cholesterol: less than 300 mg (milligrams)
- Sodium: less than 2,400 mg

On the following page, you will find Figure 2, which lists the Reference Daily Intakes (RDI), which have replaced the older Recommended Dietary Allowances (RDA). You can use these levels to calculate healthy menus for your family's meals.

Nutrient	Amount
vitamin A	5,000 International Units
vitamin C	60 milligrams (mg)
thiamin	1.5 mg
riboflavin	1.7 mg
niacin	20 mg
calcium	1.0 gram (g)
iron	18 mg
vitamin D	400 IU
vitamin E	30 IU
vitamin B6	2.0 mg
folic acid	0.4 mg
vitamin B12	6 micrograms (mcg)
phosphorus	1.0 g
iodine	150 mcg
magnesium	400 mg
zinc	15 mg
copper	2 mg
biotin	0.3 mg
pantothenic acid	10 mg

Figure 2

APPENDIX B:
MEASURES

TABLE OF STANDARD MEASUREMENTS

3 teaspoons = 1 Tablespoon

2 Tablespoons = 1 fluid ounce or 1/8 cup

4 Tablespoons = 1/4 cup

5 1/3 Tablespoons = 1/3 cup

8 Tablespoons = 1/2 cup

16 Tablespoons = 1 cup

1 cup = 8 oz. or 1/2 pint

2 pints or 4 cups = 1 quart

4 quarts (liquid) = 1 gallon

COMMON FOOD EQUIVALENTS

Bread crumbs: 3 oz. = 1 cup

Butter/shortening: 1 lb. = 2 cups

Cheese: 1 lb. = 4 cups grated

Chocolate: 1 oz. = 1 square

Coconut-shredded: 1 lb. = 6 cups

Cottage cheese: 1 lb. = 2 cups

Cranberries: 1 lb.= 4 cups

Cream cheese: 3 oz. package = 6 2/3 Tablespoons

Eggs:

- Whole: 4~6 = 1 cup
- Whites: 8~10 = 1 cup
- Yolks: 12~14 = 1 cup

Flour:

- All-purpose: 1 lb. = 4 cups, unsifted
- Cake: 1 lb. = 4 1/2 cups, unsifted
- Whole wheat: 1 lb. = 1 cup

Marshmallows: 1 lb. = 4 cups

Molasses: 1 lb. = 1 1/2 cups

Nutmeats = 1 lb = 4 cups, shelled

Raisins: 1 lb. = 2 cups, packed

Rice: 1 lb. = 2 cups, uncooked; about 6 cups cooked

Sugar:

- Brown: 1 lb. = 2 cups, firmly packed
- Confectioners: 1 lb. = 4 cups, sifted
- Granulated: 1 lb. = 2 cups

Whipping cream: 1/2 pint = 2 cups, whipped

If you want to measure partial cups by the tablespoon, remember:

4 tablespoons = 1/4 cup

5 1/3 tablespoons = 1/3 cup

8 tablespoons = 1/2 cup

10 2/3 tablespoons = 2/3 cup

12 tablespoons = 3/4 cup

14 tablespoons = 7/8 cup

OVEN TEMPERATURES

Slow: 250 to 300 Degrees

Slow moderate: 325

Moderate: 350

Quick moderate: 375

Moderately hot: 400

Hot: 425 to 450

Very hot: 475 to 500

Recipes For the Heart, Morsels For the Soul

CONTENTS OF CANS

Of the different sizes of cans used by commercial canners, the most common are:

Size	Average Contents
8 oz.	1 cup
picnic	1 1/4 cups
#300	1 3/4 cups
No. 1 tall	2 cups
No. 303	2 cups
No. 2	2 1/2 cups
No. 2 1/2	3 1/2 cups
No. 3	4 cups
No. 10	12 to 13 cups

APPENDIX C:
COMMON PAN & DISH SIZES

PAN / DISH TYPE	PAN SIZE (INCHES)	VOLUME (CUPS)
Muffin cups	1 ¾ x ¾ mini	$^1/_8$
	2 ¾ x 1 $^1/_3$	¼
	3 x 1 ¼ giant	½
Pie plates	8 x 1 ½	3
	9 x 1 ½	4
	10 x 1 ½	5
	9 x 2 (deep dish)	6
Round cake pans	8 x 1 ½	4
	8 x 2	6
	9 x 1 ½	6
	9 x 2	8
	10 x 2	11
Square cake pans	8 x 8 x 1 ½	6
	8 x 8 x 2	8
	9 x 9 x 1 ½	8
	9 x 9 x 2	10
	11 x 7 x 2	6
	13 x 9 x 2	15
Baking sheet	14 x 10	0
Jelly roll	15 ½ x 10 ½	12
Bundt	7 ½ x 3	6
	9 x 3	9
	10 x 3 ½	12
Loaf	8 ½ x 4 ½ x 2 ½	6
	9 x 5 x 3	8
Tube (angel food)	8 x 3	9
	9 x 3	12
	10 x 4	16
Springform	9 ½ x 2 ½	10
	10 x 2 ½	12

Dishes are available in the following quart sizes:
1 • 1 ½ • 2 • 2 ½ • 3

RECIPE INDEX

A

B

C

G, H, I, J, K

L

M

N, O, P

T

V

W, X, Y, Z

ABOUT THE AUTHOR...

Native Chicagoan Carol Anne Pock has always been a teacher, having spent 18 years guiding children of all ages, both inside and out of the classroom. But it wasn't until she was faced with a double-dose of frightening news — discovering first that her husband had heart disease, then that she had breast cancer — that she embarked upon her quest for a truly healthy lifestyle.

That quest has taken her to an entirely new way of looking at the foods she serves and, indeed, the very way she lives her life. With the support of her husband, Les, and her children, Jackie and Howie, she continues to teach — this time, the most fundamental lessons... of health, of happiness, and of living a joyous life.

NEED ADDITIONAL COPIES ?

**Make sure your friends and loved ones have the same
powerful morsels to live healthful, joyous lives!**

Yes, Carol! Please send me _____ additional copies of

*Recipes For The Heart,
Morsels For The Soul.*

I have enclosed a check or money order in the amount of $ _____

($17.95 each, plus $3.65 shipping & handling per copy.
Texas residents please add 8.25% sales tax to your total.)

Name: _____

Address: _____

Apartment or Suite #: _____

City: _____

State: _____ Zip: _____

Send orders and make checks payable to:
HEART & SOLE
P. O. BOX 171813
ARLINGTON, TX 76003-1813

Or call our book order department toll free at:
1-888-321-1050

Or order on-line at: www.loveyourhealth.com